ELEMENTS OF ENGLISH GRAMMAR

EEG

Rules Explained Simply

ELEMENTS OF ENGLISH GRAMMAR

Rules Explained Simply

HAROLD VAN WINKLE

MANCORP
PUBLISHING

Tampa, Florida

Book Design: Adamec Associates/Clarke Advertising, Inc.

Typesetting: Presentation Graphics

Printed in the United States of America

Library of Congress Cataloging-in-Publication Data

Van Winkle, Harold, 1906-
    Elements of English Grammar

    1. English language—Grammar—1950- I. Title
PE1112.V29   1990   428.2   89-13722
ISBN 0-931541-15-8

ACKNOWLEDGMENTS

I am indebted to Dr. Robert E. Chisnell, Professor of English, University of South Florida, for his encouragement and constructive criticism of the manuscript; to my wife Gretchen for her assistance in copyreading and proofreading; and especially to Mrs. Nancy S. White, Retired Chairman, Department of Language Arts, Booker High School, Sarasota; and to the publisher, Dr. M.N. Manougian, for their excellent comments and suggestions.

Harold Van Winkle
Bradenton, Florida

PREFACE

STANDARD ENGLISH GRAMMAR

Correct use of the language is considered a mark of intelligence and is necessary for success in most occupations. Learning the rules of grammar not only gives one confidence and a sense of pride but also an edge over others who have not mastered the language.

Some people believe there is no need to know grammar, that a person should just speak and write "naturally," but very few people "just naturally" learn the English language correctly. It requires interest and study.

This book presents the basic rules of standard English grammar in an easy-to-understand manner. It does not tell all about grammar, which would require many large volumes; but it will help you to speak and write more correctly and give you a sound basis for further study of the language.

Although all languages including English undergo changes as the years go by, standard English has become increasingly entrenched in this century. The evidence is abundant, obvious in all publishing houses where errors in grammar, spelling and usage are taboo. Standard English is a requirement in today's books, magazines, newspapers, brochures, business letters; that is, in all printed material as well as in oral presentations. Its use is a criterion by which publications as well as individuals are judged.

While there are some regional differences in pronunciation, vocabulary, and spelling in the English language, the grammar is the same everywhere. That uniformity enhances communication and has been essential in making English the most important language in the world. With serious study of the rules in this book, you can gain confidence and a better appreciation and understanding of the language you use every day.

CONTENTS

THE SENTENCE 1

PARTS OF SPEECH 61

3 CASE

4 MODIFIERS 191

5 AGREEMENT 219

6 BUILDING BETTER SENTENCES 255

ELEMENTS OF ENGLISH GRAMMAR

EEG

Rules Explained Simply

1

THE SENTENCE

The sentence is the basis of the English language, so grammar is the study of sentence structure, of the function and relationship of words that make up sentences. It is, grammatically speaking, the study of syntax, which is the way words are put together to form phrases, clauses, and sentences.

1.1 IN USE, THERE ARE FOUR KINDS OF SENTENCES.

Everyone of us has thoughts. We tell our thoughts to others by speaking or writing. When we do that, we put our thoughts into groups of words that are called sentences.

■ A *sentence* is a complete thought stated in words.

That definition itself is a sentence.

EXAMPLES

- □ It is six o'clock.
- □ When will supper be ready?
- □ Turn on the computer.
- □ I am hungry!

■ **A written sentence always begins with a capital letter, and it always ends with a punctuation mark.**

Punctuation marks inside and at the end of sentences help the reader to understand better what he or she is reading. Punctuation marks also make a difference in the meaning of a sentence, so it is important to know their proper use.

There are four kinds of sentences classified on the basis of their use or purpose. They are **declarative**, **imperative**, **interrogative**, and **exclamatory**. The mark at the end of a sentence may be a period (.), or a question mark (?), or an exclamation point (exclamation mark) (!), depending on the kind of sentence it is.

■ **A *declarative sentence* is a sentence that makes a statement, that tells something. Place a period at the end of a declarative sentence.**

EXAMPLES

- □ I am hungry.

- ☐ The office is bright.
- ☐ Ruth went to the movies.

■ An *imperative sentence* is a sentence that gives a command or tells someone to do something. Place a period or an exclamation point at the end of an imperative sentence.

EXAMPLES

- ☐ Stand there!
- ☐ Put the letter on the desk.

■ An *interrogative sentence* is a sentence that asks a question. Place a question mark at the end of an interrogative sentence.

EXAMPLES

- ☐ Are you hungry?
- ☐ When will supper be ready?

■ An *exclamatory sentence* is a sentence that expresses strong feeling, such as joy, anger, fear, surprise, or impatience. Place an exclamation point at the end of an exclamatory sentence.

EXAMPLES

- ☐ Leave me alone!
- ☐ Oh, I am sorry!

When a person speaks, his voice tells the listener whether he (the speaker) is speaking with strong emotion — whether he is angry or happy or frightened or distressed. Writing does not have that advantage, so an exclamation point is used instead. Close examination shows that an exclamatory sentence may be any one of the other three kinds of sentences.

EXAMPLE

☐ I hate dishonest people!

That kind of declarative sentence becomes an exclamatory sentence when spoken with strong feeling.

EXAMPLE

☐ Get out of my way!

That is an imperative sentence, but it becomes an exclamatory sentence when expressed with strong feeling.

EXAMPLE

☐ What are you saying!

That is an interrogative sentence that becomes an exclamatory sentence when stated with strong feeling.

Besides being used at the end of exclamatory sentences, an exclamation point may also be used after one or more words.

EXAMPLES

☐ Oh! That's what I mean.
☐ My goodness! It's a nice day.

FOR PRACTICE

Identify each sentence that follows by writing the name in the blank.

EXAMPLES

☐ I am studying grammar.   Declarative
☐ What are you studying?   Interrogative
☐ Give me an example.   Imperative
☐ It is not that easy!   Exclamatory

1. Turn on the light.   _Imperative_____
2. Can you see the rainbow?   _Interrogative_____
3. Hand it to me.   _____
4. Stop!   _____
5. The machine is now running.   _____
6. I have repaired it.   _____
7. Do you want to use it?   _____
8. It is very useful.   _____
9. Be careful!   _____
10. Take it with you.   _____

Now verify your answers.

Next test yourself by placing the correct punctuation mark at the end of each of these sentences and writing in the blank the kind of sentence it is. Then check your answers.

11. Watch out   _____
12. What are you studying   _____
13. It is a beautiful day   _____
14. Run quickly   _____
15. Are you going my way   _____
16. Anna is my sister   _____
17. I am studying grammar   _____

18.   Please bring me my book   _____

19.   He is writing a poem   _____

20.   You read the poem   _____

Now write one short sentence of each kind. Be sure to use correct punctuation marks.

Declarative   _____

Interrogative   _____

Imperative   _____

Exclamatory   _____

ANSWERS

1.	Imperative	2.	Interrogative
3.	Imperative	4.	Exclamatory
5.	Declarative	6.	Declarative
7.	Interrogative	8.	Declarative
9.	Exclamatory	10.	Imperative

11.   Watch out!   Exclamatory
12.   What are you studying?   Interrogative
13.   It is a beautiful day.   Declarative
14.   Run quickly!   Exclamatory
15.   Are you going my way?   Interrogative
16.   Anna is my sister.   Declarative
17.   I am studying grammar.   Declarative
18.   Please bring me my book. Imperative
19.   He is writing a poem.   Declarative
20.   You read the poem.   Imperative

1.2 EVERY SENTENCE HAS A SUBJECT.

You have learned that sentences may be divided into four kinds: sentences that make statements, that ask questions, that give commands, and that express strong feeling. The next step is learning the parts that make up sentences, the way sentences are constructed. The way words are arranged to form sentences and the parts of sentences is called **syntax**.

When we write or talk, we write or talk about something. In grammar what we write or talk about is called the **subject**. In each of the sentences here, the subject is in *italics*.

EXAMPLES

> The subject may be a thing.
> ☐ *The ball* rolled down the hill.
>
> The subject may be a person.
> ☐ *John* kicked the ball.
>
> The subject may be an idea.
> ☐ *Being kind to others* is a mark of civilization.

The subject is a necessary part of every sentence, but sometimes the subject is not stated. Rather, it is implied or understood without being said or written.

EXAMPLE

> ☐ Stop!

That is a sentence of only one word, but the subject is *You*. Grammatically, the sentence reads, *You stop!* Seldom is the subject stated in imperative sentences, in sentences that ask someone to do something or that give commands.

Usually it is easy to recognize the subject of a sentence if the subject is the name of a person or a thing. It is not so easy when the subject is a group of words. Here are examples with the subjects in italics.

EXAMPLES

□ *Going home* is always enjoyable.
□ *To be healthy* is my goal.
□ *Seeing her so ill* was sad.

While the subject is usually at the beginning of the sentence, that is not always true. Here are examples with the subjects in italics.

EXAMPLES

□ In the garden *flowers* were in bloom.
□ Around the room ran *the dog*.

The subject in each of these ten sentences is in italics. By studying them carefully, you will become better acquainted with the subjects of sentences.

□ *The horse* was frightened.
□ *We* need rain.
□ *Rain* fell last night.
□ *I* like ice cream.
□ *Swimming* is fun.
□ Shall *we* go there tomorrow?
□ *To drive recklessly* is dangerous.
□ Into the valley of death rode *the four hundred*.
□ By hiding in the forest, *the man* escaped being arrested.
□ *"Going My Way"* is the title of a movie.

FOR PRACTICE

Underline the subject in each of these sentences. Then check your answers.

1. Tomorrow will be a better day.

2. She will teach you.

3. Swimming is good exercise.

4. Who went to the show?

5. The teachers attended the meeting.

6. The book has a hundred pages.

7. The student is in the library.

8. The house burned.

9. My youngest brother was there.

10. Everyone was happy.

11. Listening to the speaker persuaded him to act.

12. Watching that movie was boring.

13. Into the kitchen she went happily.

14. Some were in favor of the proposition.

15. To go or not to go was the question.

ANSWERS

1.	Tomorrow	2.	She
3.	Swimming	4.	Who
5.	The teachers	6.	The book
7.	The student	8.	The house
9.	My youngest brother	10.	Everyone
11.	Listening to the speaker	12.	Watching that movie
13.	she	14.	Some
15.	To go or not to go		

1.3 EVERY SENTENCE HAS A VERB.

A sentence is a complete thought expressed in words. What the thought is about is called the **subject**, but a subject alone does not make a sentence. To be complete, the sentence must also have a **verb**. A subject and a verb are the two essential parts of every complete sentence.

■ **There are two kinds of verbs. One kind shows action; the other kind does not show action.**

EXAMPLES

☐ The ball *rolled* down the hill.
☐ John *kicked* the ball.

The verb *rolled* tells what the ball did; the verb *kicked* tells what John did. Both verbs show some kind of action.

EXAMPLES

☐ Carol *is* pretty.
☐ I *have* a book.

The verb *is* in the first sentence ties or links the word *pretty* to *Carol*. It doesn't say that Carol did anything; it just shows a condition or relationship, not any kind of movement or action. The same is true in the other sentence; there the verb *have* merely shows possession, not action. Both i*s* and *have* are examples of nonaction verbs.

EXAMPLES

1. The verbs in these sentences are in italics. Each verb shows action.

☐ The rain *fell* in torrents.
☐ The rain *soaked* the ground.

☐　The rain *flooded* the lawn.
☐　The rainwater *ran* down the roof.
☐　The rain *blew* in the window.

2.　The verbs in these sentences do not show action.

☐　They *were* happy.
☐　He *has* a car.
☐　They *have* many friends.
☐　I *am* sick.
☐　She *was* in the house.

FOR PRACTICE

Underline the verbs in these sentences.

1.　I forgot my hat.

2.　He is not angry.

3.　We worked hard.

4.　Henry came in the morning.

5.　The sky was blue yesterday.

6.　He lost his book.

7.　Cheryl studied her lesson.

8.　The children are happy.

9.　Louis built a house.

10.　William washed his hands.

Now check your answers to see how many you have underlined correctly.

It is very important in grammar to be able to recognize verbs, and it is also important to know whether a verb shows action or no action.

To test yourself, underline the verbs in these sentences. If the verb shows action, write A in the blank; if it does not show action, write N in the blank. After you have completed the list, check your answers for accuracy.

EXAMPLE

☐   She <u>chose</u> her words carefully.   A

Five of the verbs in these sentences show action; five do not.

11.   The clock struck 12 times at midnight.   _____

12.   They were in the garden.   _____

13.   The men caught several fish.   _____

14.   She had a dog with her.   _____

15.   I told him not to go.   _____

16.   The ship sank off the cape.   _____

17.   Ricky taught his brother to play the piano.   _____

18.   I have two cars.   _____

19.   Where is his home?   _____

20.   She had many admirers.   _____

Now write three short sentences with action verbs and underline the action verb in each sentence.

☐   _____

☐   _____

☐   _____

Next write three short sentences with nonaction verbs and underline the nonaction verb in each sentence.

☐   _____

☐   _____

☐   _____

<table>
<tr><td colspan="6">ANSWERS</td></tr>
</table>

1. forgot	**2.** is	**3.** worked
4. came	**5.** was	**6.** lost
7. studied	**8.** are	**9.** built
10. washed	**11.** A struck	**12.** N were
13. A caught	**14.** N had	**15.** A told
16. A sank	**17.** A taught	**18.** N have
19. N is	**20.** N had	

1.4 A VERB MAY BE MORE THAN ONE WORD.

You have learned that a verb is an essential part of a sentence; but to be able to recognize verbs, you should know that a verb may consist of more than one word.

EXAMPLES

- ☐ Mary *has baked* a cake.
- ☐ She *is baking* a cake.
- ☐ She *will be baking* a cake in the morning.
- ☐ She *had* already *baked* a cake before I arrived.
- ☐ She *will have baked* a cake by six o'clock.

In these five sentences, the word *baked* is the main part of the verb. The word or words in front of *baked* are part of the verb. They are called **helping verbs** because they help with the meaning in ways that will be explained later.*

---

* Helping verbs are also called **auxiliary verbs**. Note that forms of the verbs *to be* and *to have* are used as both helping verbs and principal verbs. Examples as helping verbs: I *was* baking a cake. I *have* baked a cake. As principal verbs: I *was* in the kitchen. I *have* a cake.

Here is a list of words commonly used as helping verbs.

have	is	be	do	may	should	am
has	was	been	does	might	would	are
had	were	can	did	could	must	will
shall						

A verb may have two, three, or even four words in it.

EXAMPLES

- □ I *study* grammar.
- □ I *am studying* grammar
- □ I *should be studying* grammar.
- □ I *should have been studying* grammar instead of watching television.

The words that form a verb are not always beside one another in the sentence. That frequently happens, especially when the word *not* is used.

EXAMPLES

- □ I *could* not *study* my lesson.
- □ I *was* not *interested* in the game.

FOR PRACTICE

Underline the verbs in these sentences.

1. She could sing beautifully.

2. He had written a letter.

3. He should drink some water.

4. I do not think so.

5. Michael will draw a picture.

6. The birds have escaped from the cage.

7. He should have been trying harder.

8. She may be studying her lesson.

9. They were eating supper.

10. She might know him.

11. I would have been pleased to win.

Now check your answers to see if you have all the verbs underlined correctly.

For practice, underline five verbs with helping verbs in an article in your newspaper or magazine. If you are in a class, the teacher may ask you to bring the article to class and read the verbs you have underlined.

You will learn more about verbs and their helping verbs in Lessons 2.6, 2.7, and 2.8.

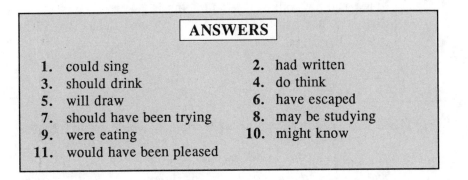

ANSWERS

1. could sing
2. had written
3. should drink
4. do think
5. will draw
6. have escaped
7. should have been trying
8. may be studying
9. were eating
10. might know
11. would have been pleased

1.5   A SENTENCE MAY HAVE MORE THAN ONE SUBJECT.

You now know that a sentence has at least one subject and one verb which together express a complete thought. You have also learned that a verb may consist of more than one word. In addition, a sentence may have more than one subject, and it may have more than one verb.

EXAMPLES

- ☐ Mary read the book.
  That sentence has one subject (Mary), and it has one verb (read).

- ☐ Mary and Jane read the book.
  That sentence has two subjects (Mary, Jane), and it has one verb (read).

- ☐ Mary and Jane read the book and talked about it.
  That sentence has two subjects (Mary, Jane), and it has two verbs (read, talked).

- ☐ Mary read the book and talked about it.
  That sentence has one subject (Mary), and it has two verbs (read, talked).

EXAMPLES

1. These sentences have two or more subjects which are in italics.

   - ☐ *The store* and *the post office* are nearby.
   - ☐ *The flowers* and *the candy* are for Helen.
   - ☐ *My uncle*, *my aunt*, and *my nephew* are visiting here.
   - ☐ *The old dog* and *the kitten* played on the rug.

2. These sentences have two or more verbs which are in italics.

   - ☐ She *played* cards and *read* books.
   - ☐ She *smiled, danced*, and *sang*.

☐ The river *rose* and *flooded* the plain.
☐ The maid *carried* in the tray and *served* coffee.
☐ She *bought* a new dress and *wore* it to the party.

In Lesson 1.2 you learned that the subject of a sentence may be more than one word, that it may be a group of words.

EXAMPLE

☐ *Wanting to take a shower* was his greatest wish.

Now in this lesson you learn that a sentence may have more than one subject, and the subjects may be groups of words. In the following example the subjects are in italics.

EXAMPLE

☐ *Attending college classes* every day and *preparing meals* at home keep me very busy.

A sentence may also have more than one verb, as you have learned, and a verb may consist of more than one word. These sentences have two verbs, each of which has more than one word.

EXAMPLES

☐ Carlos *had been working* overtime and *should have been paid* more.
☐ President Andrew Johnson *would have been impeached* in 1868 if one more senator *had voted* for it.

Identifying subjects and verbs may be difficult when you begin the study of grammar, but you should not be discouraged because it takes time to learn. All the rules will seem easier as you progress further in this book.

FOR PRACTICE

Underline the subjects in these sentences.

1. Neither Mary nor Alice went to the show.
2. John and William were honor students in high school.
3. The teacher and the coach went to the locker room.
4. Swimming and running are both good exercises.
5. Vitamins and minerals are essential for good health.

Underline the verbs in these sentences.

6. Cheryl spoke to me and smiled.
7. Each man chose a partner and danced.
8. Oscar looked in the drawer and took out a legal document.
9. Harry paid for the groceries and took them home with him.
10. The farmer planted seed, tilled the soil, and had a good harvest.

Underline the groups of words that form the subjects in these sentences.

11. Seeing her well again was a great relief.
12. To learn grammar was his goal.
13. Working full time and attending evening classes kept her very busy.
14. To get up early and to get to work on time were difficult for Maria.
15. Being at the picnic was enjoyable.

Underline the verbs in these sentences. Each has more than one word.

16. He should have arrived by now.
17. He will be arriving before noon.
18. The choir has been rehearsing all afternoon.

19. Martha is planning a surprise party.

20. She has tried to call you.

Now write a sentence that has two subjects.

☐ _____

Write a sentence that has two verbs.

☐ _____

Write a sentence that has a group of words for the subject.

☐ _____

ANSWERS

1. Mary, Alice	2. John, William
3. The teacher, the coach	4. Swimming, running
5. Vitamins, minerals	6. spoke, smiled
7. chose, danced	8. looked, took
9. paid, took	10. planted, tilled, had
11. Seeing her well again	12. To learn grammar
13. Working full time and attending evening classes	
14. To get up early and to get to work on time	
15. Being at the picnic	16. should have arrived
17. will be arriving	18. has been rehearsing
19. is planning	20. has tried

1.6 THE PREDICATE TELLS ABOUT THE SUBJECT.

■ **Every complete sentence has a subject or more than one subject. The part of the sentence not included in the subject is called the *predicate*. The predicate tells about the subject, and it always has at least one verb. In some sentences the predicate has more than one verb.**

Not only is a verb a necessary part of the predicate; in some sentences the verb may comprise the entire predicate. In the following examples the predicates are in italics.

EXAMPLES

- □   He *ran.*
- □   Leroy *smiled.*
- □   The car *stopped.*

In the following sentences the subject and the predicate are separated by a slanting line.

EXAMPLES

- □   My sister / lives in England.
- □   The Manatee River / is a mile wide in some places.
- □   Sarah / read the story to me.
- □   An invention of that kind / is worth much money.
- □   Who / saw the man in the street?

Now that you are able to recognize the complete subject and the complete predicate in sentences, you need to be able to recognize **the simple subject** and **the simple predicate.**

The subject may consist of several words, but in each subject there is a key word, or sometimes key words, that are the simple subject. The same is true of the predicate. It may consist of several words, but in every predicate there is a key word or sometimes key words that are the simple predicate. The simple predicate is, of course, always a verb.

EXAMPLES

- □   The baseball *team / needs* a new coach.
  The complete subject in that sentence is *The baseball team;* the simple subject is *team.* The complete predicate in that sentence is *needs a new coach;* the simple predicate is *needs.*

☐   The Houston *voters* / *went* to the polls today to elect a mayor.
In that sentence the simple subject is *voters*; the simple predicate is *went*.

☐   *Tim Johnson*, who is my cousin, / *was elected* chairman of the committee.
In that sentence the simple subject is *Tim Johnson*; the simple predicate is *was elected*.

■   **Every verb in a sentence has a subject.**

Being able to recognize simple subjects and simple predicates is a great help in determining the subject of a verb; and being able to determine the subjects of verbs is an essential part of grammar.

FOR PRACTICE

As you have learned to recognize subjects and verbs, separating the subject from the predicate should be easy. Draw a slanting line to separate the subject from the predicate in each of these sentences. Then check your answers to see if you have them marked correctly.

1. The smell of cooking bacon made me hungry.
2. He worried about his brother's illness.
3. The problem was easy for Louise.
4. The caged lion stared at us.
5. My brother bought four loaves of bread.

Now see if you can separate the subject from the predicate in each of these longer sentences. Two of them contain more than one subject; three contain more than one verb.

6. My sister Estrala and her cousin Nina went to the mall yesterday.

7. The old man walked down the street and entered a dingy restaurant.

8. The cook went to the market on Thursday and bought vegetables.

9. Playing tennis and swimming were his chief activities.

10. Henry won the race and was awarded a trophy.

For further practice, write a sentence for each of these subjects and verbs and separate the subject from the predicate in each sentence with a slanting line. (The name of the slanting line of that kind is *slash* or *virgule*.)

	Subject	Verb
11.	No one	saw
12.	You	dropped
13.	Jeff	is
14.	The clouds	were
15.	The flowers in the garden	have

■ **Review: The subject is what the sentence (a complete thought) is about. The predicate tells something about the subject. Every predicate has one or more verbs. There are two kinds of verbs: one shows action; the other only indicates a relationship or a condition.**

Underline the simple subjects and the simple predicates in these sentences.

16. The price of copper soared last Thursday.

17. The investor in stocks could use some of that information.

18. Indiana University offers degrees in numerous areas of study.

19. The pastry cook made a beautiful marble cake.

20. Seven students were reading in the basement room.

ANSWERS

1. The smell of cooking bacon / made me hungry.
2. He / worried about his brother's illness.
3. The problem / was easy for Louise.
4. The caged lion / stared at us.
5. My brother / bought four loaves of bread.
6. My sister and her cousin Nina / went to the mall yesterday.
7. The old man / walked down the street and entered a dingy restaurant.
8. The cook / went to the market and bought vegetables.
9. Playing tennis and swimming / were his chief activities.
10. Henry / won the race and was awarded a trophy.
16. price / soared
17. investor / could use
18. Indiana University / offers
19. cook / made
20. students / were reading

1.7 TWO OR MORE SENTENCES MAY BE WRITTEN AS ONE.

The sentences you have studied so far are called **simple sentences** because they express one complete thought. Often when we speak or write, we connect two or more simple sentences (two or more complete thoughts) together, usually with a connecting word or words. Two or more simple sentences written as one are called a **compound sentence**.

EXAMPLES

The connecting words are in italics.

☐ The boy came to our house early, *but* he did not stay long.
☐ I will go there tomorrow, *or* I will not go at all.

□ The women rode in carriages, *and* the men walked behind them.

□ He ate rapidly, *for* he was very hungry.

□ Rose went shopping *and* Mary went with her, *but* they did not buy anything.

Note that there is a complete sentence on either side of the connecting word in each of those compound sentences. For example, the first could be read as two sentences. *The boy came. He did not stay.* Note also that a compound sentence may be formed by combining more than two sentences, as shown in the last example above. It contains three sentences.

The word *compound* means something formed by combining parts. In grammar *compound* refers not only to sentences but also to words and word groups. For example, you have learned that a simple sentence may have more than one subject, and it may have more than one verb. These sentences below illustrate a compound subject, a compound predicate (two verbs), and a compound sentence.

| EXAMPLES |

□ *The store and the post office* are nearby.
Compound subject.

□ The river *rose and flooded* the plain.
Compound predicate.

□ *I can walk to the store*, or *I can ride my bike*.
Compound sentence.

FOR PRACTICE

Underline the connecting word between the simple sentences in each of these compound sentences.

1. He didn't like spinach, yet he ate it.

2. It had been a long day, and we were very tired.

3. I went to the circus, but Emilio stayed home.

4. The water was bitter, so he didn't drink it.

5. Carla took a shovel with her to the garden, but she could not find the rake.

It is important to be able to distinguish between compound sentences and simple sentences that have compound subjects or compound predicates. In the blanks below, write C if the sentence is compound and S if the sentence is simple with a compound subject or a compound predicate.

6. ___ Mary and Jane were working in the garden.

7. ___ Mary worked hard, but Jane often sat and rested.

8. ___ The roses needed food, so they worked fertilizer in the soil around the roots.

9. ___ The roses grew rapidly and blossomed profusely.

10. ___ The girls picked a basket of flowers, yet many still remained on the bushes.

11. ___ Both flowers and vegetables grew in the garden.

12. ___ We sold vegetables, but we kept the flowers for ourselves.

13. ___ I like cabbage and carrots, so I planted a large crop.

14. ___ Worms and insects damaged some of the plants.

15. ___ Tilling the soil carefully and watering the plants in dry weather produced a good crop of vegetables and flowers.

Now check your answers to see how many you have marked correctly.

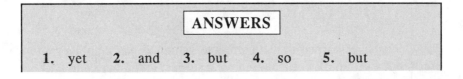

ANSWERS

1. yet   2. and   3. but   4. so   5. but

The aim in this lesson is to learn to distinguish between simple and compound sentences. Note that in each of the sentences 1 through 5 there is a simple sentence on either side of the connecting word. The sentences 6 through 15 are more difficult. Here are the answers.

6. _S_ This is a simple sentence with a compound subject. The subject is *Mary and Jane.*

7. _C_ This is a compound sentence with two simple sentences connected by the word *but*.

8. _C_ This is also a compound sentence with two simple sentences connected by the word *so*.

9. _S_ This is a simple sentence with a compound predicate. The two verbs forming the predicate are *grew* and *blossomed.*

10. _C_ This is a compound sentence formed by two simple sentences connected by the word *yet*.

11. _S_ This is a simple sentence with a compound subject. The two subjects are *flowers* and *vegetables*.

12. _C_ This is a compound sentence formed by two simple sentences connected by the word *but*.

13. _C_ This is a compound sentence formed by two simple sentences connected by the word *so*.

14. _S_ This is a simple sentence with a compound subject, The two subjects are *Worms* and *insects*.

15. _S_ This is a simple sentence with a compound subject. The two subjects are *Tilling the soil* and *watering the plants*.

1.8 A DEPENDENT CLAUSE IS NOT A COMPLETE SENTENCE.

You have learned that a complete sentence has a subject and a verb; but a group of words may have a subject and a verb and still not express a complete thought. It may not be a complete sentence grammatically.

□ If he comes home . . .
□ When I find the book . . .
□ After he is elected . . .

Each of these examples leaves the reader asking, "Then what happens?" They are not complete sentences (not complete thoughts). To make them complete sentences, they may be written this way:

□ *I will tell him* if he comes home.
□ When I find the book, *I will read it.*
□ After he is elected, *he will have an office.*

The part of each of those sentences in italics is in itself a complete sentence and is called an **independent clause.*** The part not in italics, which cannot stand alone as a complete sentence, is called a **dependent clause.**

■ **A sentence that contains an independent clause and one or more dependent clauses is called a *complex sentence.***

The following are complex sentences with the dependent clauses in italics.

□ I asked *who went with him.*
□ *Although I was only ten years old,* I traveled alone.
□ The boat *that has a leak* is of little value.
□ The poem, *which was published yesterday,* is beautiful.
□ *Unless he is sick,* he will come to the meeting.

---

* An independent clause may also be called a **main clause** or a **principal clause.**
A dependent clause may also be called a **subordinate clause.**

EXAMPLES

The following are complex sentences with subjects and verbs in dependent clauses in italics.

☐ I asked him if *he wanted* to go.
The independent clause is *I asked him.* In the dependent clause the subject is *he* and the verb is *wanted.*

☐ Although *I was* only ten years old, I traveled alone.
The independent clause is *I traveled alone.* In the dependent clause the subject is *I* and the verb is *was.*

☐ The boat *that has* a leak is of little value.
The independent clause is *The boat is of little value.* In the dependent clause the subject is *that* and the verb is *has.*

☐ The poem, *which was published* yesterday, is beautiful.
The independent clause is *The poem is beautiful.* In the dependent clause the subject is *which* and the verb is *was published.*)

☐ Unless *he is* sick, he will come to the meeting.
The independent clause is *he will come to the meeting.* In the dependent clause the subject is *he* and the verb is *is.*

FOR PRACTICE

In grammar it is necessary to be able to tell whether a group of words with a subject and a verb is or is not a complete sentence. Read the ten sentences below and place the letter I (for incomplete) in the blank if the group of words is not a compete sentence and the letter C if the group is a complete sentence. There are five of each.

1. Because she was tired.   _____
2. Until he arrived.   _____
3. Did you eat your supper?   _____
4. Since I arrived home.   _____

5. Unless it rains, we will be there.   _____

6. Wherever you go.   _____

7. Susie laughed.   _____

8. Where are you going?   _____

9. When the sun shines.   _____

10. He wore a brown coat.   _____

Now check your answers.

Underline the dependent clauses in these complex sentences.

11. If I had money, I would go to Europe.

12. Although he was of legal age, he did not vote.

13. I go to the gym whenever I can.

14. He washed his hands before he ate the sandwich.

15. The man who lives on the hill is my uncle.

16. Our car, which we bought yesterday, is a Buick.

17. He ate until he was no longer hungry.

18. I will go wherever you wish.

19. Mary danced while John played the guitar.

20. He rested because he was tired.

Now check your answers.

ANSWERS

Numbers 3, 5, 7, 8, and 10 are complete sentences and should be marked with the letter C. The letter I goes in the blanks for 1, 2, 4, 6, and 9 because they are incomplete sentences. To make them complete, they can be written as follows.

1. She stopped because she was tired.
   (*She stopped* is the independent clause; *because she was tired* is the dependent clause.)
2. Until he arrived, we waited in the house.
   (*we waited in the house* is the independent clause; *Until he arrived* is the dependent clause.)
4. I have not seen her since I arrived home.
   (*I have not seen her* is the independent clause; *since I arrived home* is the dependent clause.)
6. Wherever you go, I will follow.
   (*I will follow* is the independent clause; *Wherever you go* is the dependent clause.)
9. When the sun shines, we go to the beach.
   (*we go to the beach* is the independent clause; *When the sun shines* is the dependent clause.)

To repeat, a dependent clause is a group of words that has a subject and a verb but is not a complete sentence; it must be accompanied by an independent clause for the sentence to be complete. A sentence that contains an independent clause and a dependent clause is called a *complex sentence*.

Complex sentences with dependent clauses in italics.

11. *If I had money*, I would go to Europe.
12. *Although he was of legal age*, he did not vote.
13. I go to the gym *whenever I can.*
14. He washed his hands *before he ate the sandwich.*
15. The man *who lives on the hill* is my uncle.
16. Our car, *which we bought yesterday*, is a Buick.
17. He ate *until he was no longer hungry.*
18. I will go *wherever you wish.*
19. Mary danced *while John played the guitar.*
20. He rested *because he was tired.*

1.9 IN STRUCTURE, THERE ARE FOUR KINDS OF SENTENCES.

You have learned three kinds of sentences according to structure. They are *simple sentences*, *compound sentences*, and *complex sentences*. Here is a review plus an introduction to the fourth kind, the compound-complex sentence.

■ **A *simple sentence* is a group of words that expresses a complete thought. It always contains a subject and a verb, and it may contain more than one subject and more than one verb.**

EXAMPLES

- ☐ Maria is my sister.
  (one subject, one verb)
- ☐ Maria and Elena live in Boston.
  (two subjects, one verb)
- ☐ They live together and work in the same office.
  (one subject, two verbs)

■ **A *compound sentence* is two, or more than two, simple sentences written as one. The sentences are usually but not always joined by a connecting word or words.**

A simple sentence + a simple sentence = a compound sentence.

EXAMPLE

- ☐ Maria is my sister, and Elena is my cousin.

A simple sentence + a simple sentence + a simple sentence = a compound sentence.

EXAMPLE

- ☐ Maria is my sister, Elena is my cousin, and Joe is my brother.

■   A *complex sentence* contains an independent clause (a simple sentence) and a dependent clause. It may contain more than one dependent clause. The independent clause and the dependent clause each has a subject and a verb.

A simple sentence + a dependent clause = a complex sentence.

EXAMPLE

☐   Maria, who lives in Boston, is my sister.

A simple sentence + a dependent clause + a dependent clause =
a complex sentence.

EXAMPLE

☐   Maria, who works in Boston and who is my sister, lives with her cousin Elena.

■   A fourth kind of sentence in structure is the *compound-complex sentence*. It is formed when a simple sentence and a complex sentence, or two or more complex sentences, are connected to form a longer sentence.

A simple sentence + a complex sentence = a compound-complex
sentence.

EXAMPLES

☐   She gave me a present, but *when I saw it* I was not happy. (The dependent clause is in italics.)

☐   Delaware, *which was named for Lord De La Warr, an early governor of Virginia*, was the first of the original 13 states to ratify the U.S. Constitution in 1787; but Connecticut is known as the "Constitution State."

A complex sentence + a complex sentence = a compound-complex
sentence.

EXAMPLE

□ *When I came home* I cooked supper, and Henry didn't look
so tired *after he had eaten.*
(The dependent clauses are in italics.)

Here are more sentences to illustrate better the four kinds in regard
to structure.

EXAMPLES

1. Simple Sentences

□ Henry went to the beach.
(One subject, *Henry*, and one verb, *went*)

□ Henry and Sam walked to the beach.
(Two subjects, *Henry*, *Sam*, and one verb, *walked*)

□ Henry walked to the beach and swam in the ocean.
(One subject, *Henry*, and two verbs, *walked*, *swam*)

□ Henry and Sam walked to the beach and swam in the ocean.
(Two subjects, *Henry*, *Sam*, and two verbs, *walked*, *swam*)

Write a simple sentence of your own.

□ _____

2. Compound Sentences

□ Henry walked to the beach, but he did not swim in the ocean.
(Two simple sentences connected by the word *but*)

□ Henry and Sam walked to the ocean, and they swam in the
ocean.
(Two simple sentences connected by the word *and*. The first
of the two simple sentences has a compound subject, *Henry
and Sam.*)

Write a compound sentence of your own.

□ _____

3. Complex Sentence

☐ Henry and Sam walked to the beach where they swam in the ocean.
(The independent clause is *Henry and Sam walked to the beach.* The dependent clause is *where they swam in the ocean.*)

Write a complex sentence of your own.

☐ _____

4. Compound-Complex Sentence

☐ Henry and Sam walked to the beach where Henry swam in the ocean, but Sam just sat and watched.
(Here a complex sentence and a simple sentence are combined to form a compound-complex sentence. The simple sentence is *Sam just sat and watched.* The sentence before the connecting word *but* is complex. The independent clause is *Henry and Sam walked to the beach.* The dependent clause is *where Henry swam in the ocean.*)

Write a compound-complex sentence of your own.

☐ _____

FOR PRACTICE

To test yourself, underline the words that connect simple sentences to form compound sentences.

1. I tried to talk to her, but she would not listen.
2. She threw the ball, and her friend caught it.
3. He had to have the money, or he could not make the trip.
4. He had the money, yet he would not make the trip.
5. I dreaded to go, for it is a difficult journey.

Now underline the dependent clauses in these complex sentences.

6. I will go wherever you go.
7. If I lose the bet, I will pay you.
8. When autumn arrives, we will go to Florida.
9. Mr. Smith, who owns a farm in Alabama, lives next door to us.
10. These apples, which she loves, come from Oregon.

Here are five compound-complex sentences. Underline the dependent clauses in each. There is one dependent clause in each of the first four sentences; two dependent clauses in the fifth.

11. She will sing a solo if you ask her; however, she doesn't really want to sing.
12. She explained carefully where the house is; still, I could not find it.
13. He was always on hand when we needed him, yet we seldom asked him for help.
14. He swam in the river every morning when the weather was warm, and in winter he exercised indoors.
15. He asked where I had been; and when I told him, he was surprised.

Check yourself by writing in the blank by each sentence below whether the sentence is simple, complex, compound, or compound-complex.

16. He went to bed, but he did not sleep. _____
17. He went to bed and slept. _____
18. He went to bed while I was reading, but he did not sleep well. _____
19. He went to bed while I was reading, but he did not sleep well because he was troubled. _____
20. She stopped because she was tired. _____

21. Mary and Alice went to the market and shopped for groceries. _____

22. After I gave them some money, Mary and Alice went to the market and shopped for food. _____

23. When we saw what they had purchased, we were pleased. _____

24. Charles came to see me when I was ill; however, I did not want to see him. _____

25. When she arrives, we will ask her. _____

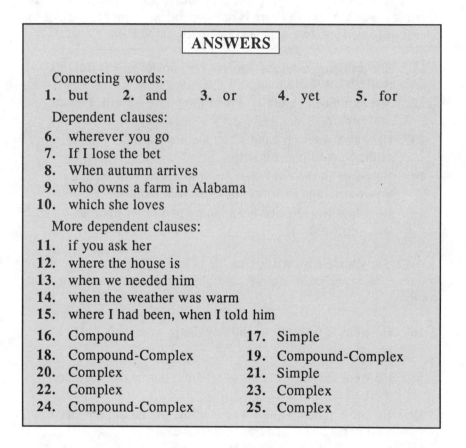

ANSWERS

Connecting words:
1. but   2. and   3. or   4. yet   5. for

Dependent clauses:
6. wherever you go
7. If I lose the bet
8. When autumn arrives
9. who owns a farm in Alabama
10. which she loves

More dependent clauses:
11. if you ask her
12. where the house is
13. when we needed him
14. when the weather was warm
15. where I had been, when I told him

16. Compound   17. Simple
18. Compound-Complex   19. Compound-Complex
20. Complex   21. Simple
22. Complex   23. Complex
24. Compound-Complex   25. Complex

1.10 CONNECTIVES ARE COMMON WORDS WE USE EVERY DAY.

Six kinds of connectives are used in the sentences we speak and write. Two kinds are used to join or connect dependent clauses to independent clauses to form complex sentences. They are **subordinating conjunctions** and **relative pronouns** and are discussed in the next lesson.

Four kinds of connectives are used to form compound and compound-complex sentences. **Coordinating conjunctions, correlative conjunctions, conjunctive adverbs,** and **transitional phrases** are discussed here.

■ **Coordinating conjunctions***

and   but   or   for   so   yet   nor

The word *coordinate* means equal rank; a coordinating conjunction is thus used to connect or link not only sentences but also words and groups of words of equal rank.

EXAMPLES

☐ Sally and John were talking.
   In that sentence the coordinating conjunction *and* connects two words of equal rank; together the two words form the compound subject of that simple sentence.

☐ The wind blew and shook the house.
   In that sentence the coordinating conjunction *and* connects two verbs of equal rank, *blew* and *shook*, in a simple sentence.

☐ He asked me a question, *but* I could not answer it.
   In that sentence the conjunction *but* connects two simple sentences to form a compound sentence.

---

* In grammar a conjunction is one or more words that join words, groups of words, and sentences. Conjunctions as a part of speech are explained more fully in Lesson 2.18.

■ **Correlative conjunctions** (always used in pairs)

both . . . and   not only . . . but also
either . . . or   whether . . . or
neither . . . nor   just as . . . so

EXAMPLES

□ *Either* he will pay me, *or* I will sue him.
□ *Whether* he goes *or* whether he stays will not make any
   difference.
□ *Just as* he does many good deeds, *so* does he also make
   many friends.
□ *Neither* Henry *nor* James had any money.

In the first three sentences correlative conjunctions are used to
connect simple sentences to form compound sentences. In the fourth
sentence the correlative conjunction is used to connect two subjects in
a simple sentence.

■ **Conjunctive adverbs**

The following words are called **conjunctive adverbs** when they
are used as connectives between two or more independent clauses to
form compound sentences.

accordingly	however	now
also	incidentally	next
anyway	indeed	similarly
besides	instead	still
certainly	likewise	then
consequently	meanwhile	thereafter
finally	moreover	therefore

furthermore	nevertheless	thus
hence	otherwise	undoubtedly
nonetheless		

EXAMPLE

□ I have never had a million dollars; *therefore*, I am unable to say what I would do if I were wealthy.

■ **Transitional phrases. Sometimes two or more words, called** *transitional phrases*,* **are used as connectives to tie or link sentences together. These are commonly used.**

that is	in order that	at any rate
what is more	even so	in fact
after all	for example	in addition
at the same time	on the other hand	in that
as if	in other words	no matter how
as soon as	on the contrary	so that
as though		

EXAMPLES

□ We assured John that his mistake has caused us no difficulty; *even so*, he felt bad about it.
□ He said he was not a thaumaturgist; *in other words*, he meant that he could not perform magic that would right the situation.

---

* A **phrase** is a group of two or more grammatically related words without a subject or a verb. There are several kinds. They are explained more fully in Lessons 2.17, 4.5, and 4.6.

This lesson presents essentially two kinds or classifications of connectives. One kind is *coordinating* and *correlative* conjunctions; the other kind is *conjunctive adverbs* and *transitional phrases*. The lists are not complete. The distinction between the two kinds has little if any grammatical significance; but the distinction is important in regard to punctuation.

Punctuation, to be explained in another lesson, is as much a part of language as words are. Each punctuation mark serves a particular function in communication just as each word does.

1.11   THERE ARE TWO KINDS OF CONNECTIVES FOR DEPENDENT CLAUSES.

Just as one or more connective words are used to connect sentences to form compound and compound-complex sentences, as shown in the previous lesson, so also are connective words used to connect dependent clauses to independent clauses to form complex sentences. There are two kinds, **subordinating conjunctions** and **relative pronouns**, and they differ in construction.

■   **Subordinating conjunctions. The words below are used to connect dependent clauses to independent clauses in complex sentences. They are called subordinating conjunctions.**

if	after	while
although	before	where
since	until	wherever
because	when	once
unless	whenever	as
that	provided that	whether

EXAMPLES

The subordinating conjunctions are in italics.

□   *If* I can earn enough money, I will buy a car.

□   I will buy a car *if* I can earn enough money.

■   **Relative pronouns. When the words below are used to introduce dependent clauses in complex sentences, they are relative pronouns.**

who	that	whomever
whom	which	whichever
whose	what	whatever
whoever		

EXAMPLES

□   A man *who* betrays his country is a traitor.

□   A horse *that* is gentle is a pleasure to ride.

The difference in those two groups of words is that subordinating conjunctions **connect** dependent or subordinate clauses to independent or main clauses while relative pronouns **introduce** dependent or subordinate clauses. Another way of explaining the difference is that dependent clauses introduced by relative pronouns generally refer to the subject while those connected by subordinating conjunctions usually refer to the verb. This is explained more fully in Lesson 4.3.

FOR PRACTICE

Fill in the blanks with the letter S if the word in italics in the dependent clause is a subordinating conjunction and the letter R if it is a relative pronoun. There are five of each.

1. __ I will go *wherever* you go.

2. __ Make hay *while* the sun shines.

3. __ The man *who* mows our lawn lives on a farm.

4. __ *After* I have supper, I will go to the theater.

5. __ The display *that* won the prize was designed by my father.

6. __ That dog, *which* is a terrier, is seven years old.

7. __ I remained indoors *because* it was raining.

8. __ The woman *whose* car was damaged is my aunt.

9. __ The date was chosen *after* we had taken a vote.

10. __ The date *that* was chosen is May 3.

Then check your answers to see how well you have done.

Suggestion: In school, students are taught to read for meaning. Now as you are learning grammar it would help you to study the structure of sentences as well as reading for content. With a pencil or pen, underline some independent and dependent clauses and conjunctions as you read your newspaper. If you are in class, your teacher may ask you to bring some of the examples with you.

ANSWERS

1. S	2. S	3. R	4. S	5. R
6. R	7. S	8. R	9. S	10. R

1.12 PUNCTUATION IS AN ESSENTIAL PART OF WRITTEN COMMUNICATION.

In the very first lesson you learned the punctuation marks to use at the end of sentences. The use of punctuation marks inside sentences is more complicated. To use them correctly, you must be able to recognize independent and dependent clauses.

The principal rule for punctuating compound and compound-complex sentences internally requires the use of two punctuation marks. A semicolon goes before conjunctive adverbs and transitional phrases that connect or join independent clauses. A comma goes before coordinating conjunctions and correlative conjunctions that connect or join independent clauses. More specifically, here are four rules.

■ **Rule. Use a semicolon (;) before, and generally a comma after, a conjunctive adverb or a transitional phrase in a compound sentence.**

EXAMPLE

□ The Pirates used four pitchers in nine innings in trying to win the ball game; *however*, they lost by a large score.
(The conjunctive adverb is in italics.)

EXAMPLE

□ He maintained that the building he was proposing would be an asset to the community; *in addition*, he offered to resurface the street at no cost to the city.
(The transitional phrase is in italics.)

Note that a semicolon is always used *before* a conjunctive adverb and a transitional phrase, and generally a comma *after*.

■ **Rule. Use a comma (,) between independent clauses when they are connected or joined by a coordinating conjunction or a correlative conjunction.**

EXAMPLE

□ I spent the afternoon at the ball park watching the Pirates play baseball, *but* Clara stayed home to take a nap.
(The coordinating conjunction is in italics.)

A short compound sentence may not need internal punctuation.

□   I talked and she listened.

On the other hand, a semicolon rather than a comma may be used if the compound sentence is especially long and the thoughts in the sentences are in contrast.

□   The country has beautiful scenery and abundant natural re-
sources; but many people in that land live in abject poverty.

■   **Rule. Use a semicolon before a coordinating conjunction or correlative conjunction in a compound sentence that has internal punctuation.**

□   We ran to the beach, swam in the water, and lay in the sun;
but we should have been at the office, because there was
much urgent work to be done there.

Because of internal punctuation (commas) in that sentence, a semicolon is needed before the coordinating conjunction.

■   **Rule. A compound sentence written without a connecting word or words must be punctuated with a semicolon, not a comma.**

□   She was easily pleased; she liked everything in the house.
(correct)

☐   She was happy at home; she liked being alone.
(correct)

☐   She was happy at home, she liked being alone.
(incorrect)

To the student: Can you explain why that sentence is punctuated incorrectly?

FOR PRACTICE

Punctuate these sentences correctly.

1.   I threw the ball and Richard caught it.

2.   I threw the ball as gently as I could but John was unable to catch it.

3.   I threw the ball John was unable to catch it.

4.   She spoke and the audience listened.

5.   I had wanted all my life to travel however I found it necessary to stay at home.

6.   He had all the facts needed to win the case what is more he was willing to disclose them to the court.

7.   The rain fell all day long the playing field was covered with water.

8.   When I saw him yesterday, he promised to pay the rent today but didn't what is more he still owes for the use of the car last week.

9.   When the sun came out this morning after a hard rain, I had an urge to go for a long walk yet when I thought about all the work that needed to be done, I remained in the office.

10.   I looked all about me in the woods and in the fields and I saw the beauty of nature wherever I looked.

11.   I found the students busy at their desks and the teacher grading papers.

12. Michael, who is my cousin, says he loves to travel however he seldom goes anywhere.

13. He has talked about taking a long voyage still I never expect him to do so.

14. When I asked him why he didn't take a trip he was evasive.

15. If he does decide to go, I will be happy furthermore I will pay his expenses if he doesn't have enough money.

Now check your punctuation with the sentences below to see if you have done it correctly. Study the explanations to understand the reasons.

ANSWERS

1. This compound sentence is so short that no internal punctuation is needed.

2. I threw the ball as gently as I could, but John was unable to catch it.
   (In a longer compound sentence, use a comma before the coordinating conjunction — provided the sentence has no internal punctuation, and this one doesn't.)

3. I threw the ball; John was unable to catch it.
   (Use a semicolon between the two sentences in a compound sentence that has no conjunction connecting the two sentences.)

4. She spoke and the audience listened.
   (This compound sentence is so short it needs no internal punctuation.)

5. I wanted all my life to travel; however, I found it necessary to stay at home.
   (Place a semicolon before and a comma after a conjunctive adverb in a compound sentence.)

6. He had all the facts he needed to win the case; what is more, he was willing to disclose them to the court.
   (A semicolon goes before and a comma after a transitional phrase in a compound sentence.)

7. The rain fell all day long; the playing field was covered with water.
    (Use a semicolon in a compound sentence that has no conjunction. This is the same as number 3 above.)

8. When I saw him yesterday, he promised to pay the rent today but didn't; what is more, he still owes for use of the car last week.
    (Use a semicolon before and a comma after a transitional phrase in a compound sentence. Here the transitional phrase is *what is more.*)

9. When the sun came out this morning after a hard rain, I had an urge to go for a long walk; yet, when I thought about all the work that needed to be done, I remained in the office.
    (This compound sentence has internal punctuation, so a semicolon goes before *yet* and a comma after.)

10. I looked all about me in the woods and in the fields, and I saw the beauty of nature wherever I looked.
    (A comma goes before the coordinating conjunction in a long compound sentence that has no internal punctuation.)

11. I found the students writing at their desks and the teacher grading papers.
    (This is a simple sentence with a compound predicate. No internal punctuation is needed.)

12. Michael, who is my cousin, says he loves to travel; however, he seldom goes anywhere.
    (Use a semicolon before and a comma after a conjunctive adverb in a compound sentence.)

13. He has talked about taking a long voyage; still, I never expect him to do so.
    (Use a semicolon before and a comma after a conjunctive adverb in a compound sentence.)

14. When I asked him why he didn't take a trip, he was evasive.
    (This is a complex sentence, not a compound sentence. The comma is used to separate a subordinate clause out of its natural order from the rest of the sentence.)

15. If he does decide to go, I will be happy; furthermore, I will pay his expenses if he doesn't have enough money.
    (Use a semicolon before and a comma after a conjunctive adverb in a compound sentence.)

1.13 COMMAS MAKE A DIFFERENCE IN THE MEANING.

A complex sentence, as you know, has an independent clause and one or more dependent clauses. A comma is generally used to separate the dependent clause from the independent clause when the dependent clause comes first in the sentence; that is to say, when it is "out of its natural order."

EXAMPLE

☐ *When I saw it*, I was surprised.
(The dependent clause is in italics.)

When the sentence is written with the dependent clause last, no comma is needed. It would then read this way.

☐ I was surprised *when I saw it*.

There are instances when the use of commas to separate the subordinate clause from the main clause makes a difference in meaning, and this is important to know.

EXAMPLES

☐ The man, *who was our guide*, was pleasant.
(With commas)
☐ The man *who was our guide* was pleasant.
(Without commas)

The first sentence, with commas, simply tells that our guide was a pleasant man. The second sentence, without the commas, implies that there was more than one man and of them, our guide, was pleasant. The implication is that the others were not pleasant.

The dependent clause in the first sentence, separated from the rest of the sentence by commas, is called a **nonrestrictive clause**. That means that it is not necessary to the meaning of the sentence; it merely adds information to the sentence.

The dependent clause in the second sentence, the one with no commas, is called a **restrictive clause** because it is essential to the complete meaning of the sentence.

■ **Rule. Separate a nonrestrictive clause from the rest of the sentence with commas; do not separate a restrictive clause from the rest of the sentence with commas.**

EXAMPLES

☐ The teacher read to the students, *who had low grades*. (Nonrestrictive)
☐ The teacher read to the students *who had low grades*. (Restrictive)

The first sentence, with the nonrestrictive clause, means that all the students the teacher read to had low grades. The second sentence means that the teacher read to those who had low grades but not to those who had higher grades. In other words, the second sentence implies that there were two groups of students, those with low grades and those with higher grades, and the teacher read only to those who had the low grades.

Three relative pronouns should be mentioned here in connection with restrictive and nonrestrictive clauses. They are *who*, *which*, and *that*.

■ **When there is a choice between *that* and *which*, *that* is generally used to introduce restrictive clauses and *which* is generally used to introduce nonrestrictive clauses.**

EXAMPLES

☐ This is the house *that* burned yesterday.
☐ The flowers *that* filled the garden were beautiful.

EXAMPLES

- ☐ My house, *which* is near the river, has a large front porch.
- ☐ Ocean perch, *which* is delicious, is one of my favorite foods.

■ **The relative pronouns *who* and *that* are generally used to refer to persons while the pronoun *which* is used to refer to animals and things.**

EXAMPLES

- ☐ The man *who* gave me the pencil is my teacher.
- ☐ The man *that* stopped us is a policeman.
- ☐ His home, *which* burned yesterday, was not insured.
- ☐ My dog, *which* I like very much, is a Dalmation.

Here is another example of restrictive vs. nonrestrictive clauses for you to study.

Nonrestrictive

- ☐ My uncle, who lives on the hill, is a carpenter.

That sentence states only that my uncle is a carpenter. That he lives on a hill is merely an additional piece of information, not essential to the meaning of the sentence. It could just as well be two sentences: My uncle is a carpenter. He lives on a hill.

Restrictive

- ☐ My uncle who lives on the hill is a carpenter.

Here the dependent clause, without the commas, changes the meaning. It implies that I have more than one uncle, and the one who lives on the hill is a carpenter. Any other uncles I have are not carpenters.

■ **Another rule requires that the name of a person addressed in writing be separated from the rest of the sentence by a comma or commas.** *

Here, again, the use of a comma can make a difference in the meaning. Suppose you address Mr. Anderson.

EXAMPLES

☐ Mr. Anderson, a successful farmer once lived here.

In that sentence you tell Mr. Anderson that a successful farmer once lived here. Now read the sentence with a comma after the word *farmer*.

☐ Mr. Anderson, a successful farmer, once lived here.

By adding the comma, the words *a successful farmer* merely tell something about Mr. Anderson. The sentence now states that Mr. Anderson was a successful farmer and that he no longer lives here.

The sentence may also be written with a nonrestrictive clause.

☐ Mr. Anderson, who was a successful farmer, once lived here.

Or it may be written as direct address with the name of the person addressed inside the sentence.

☐ Yes, Mr. Anderson, a successful farmer once lived here.

---

* This book is primarily about grammar and therefore does not contain all the rules for punctuation. Complete rules for punctuation and capitalization can be found in all English handbooks and in the Manual of Style in large dictionaries.

Among recommended handbooks are *The Holt Handbook*, published by Holt, Rinehart and Winston, 1986, and *Harbrace College Handbook*, published by Harcourt Brace Jovanovich, Inc., 1982.

FOR PRACTICE

Check yourself by punctuating these sentences correctly with commas.

1. Complex sentence with the dependent clause at the end.

   ☐ We went home after we had waited for hours

2. Complex sentence with the dependent clause out of its natural order.

   ☐ After we had waited for hours we went home.

3. Direct address: speaking to someone and calling her by name.

   ☐ Edith can you go tomorrow?

4. Complex sentence with a restrictive clause.

   ☐ The house that burned was old.

5. Complex sentence with a nonrestrictive clause.

   ☐ The house which burned was old.

6. Direct address.

   ☐ I wish Mary you would go with us tomorrow.

7. Complex sentence with a restrictive clause.

   ☐ The dog that barked is a collie.

8. Complex sentence with a nonrestrictive clause.

   ☐ The dog which barked is a collie.

9. Complex sentence with a restrictive clause.

   ☐ The company hired the men who had gone to college.

10. Complex sentence with a nonrestrictive clause.

   ☐ The company hired the men who had gone to college.

Now check your answers to see how many you have right. Remember to study the explanations.

ANSWERS

1. We went home after we had waited for hours.
    (No internal punctuation needed.)
2. After we had waited for hours, we went home.
    (Comma needed after the dependent clause out of its
    natural order.)
3. Edith, can you go with us tomorrow?
    (Comma after person spoken to.)
4. The house that burned was old.
    (No internal punctuation needed. The sentence implies
    that the house that did not burn wasn't old.)
5. The house, which burned, was old.
    (Nonrestrictive clause, which merely gives additional in-
    formation but is not essential to the meaning is separated
    from the rest of the sentence by commas.)
6. I wish, Mary, you would go with us tomorrow.
    (Person spoken to separated from the rest of the sentence
    by commas.)
7. The dog that barked is a collie.
    (No commas needed for a restrictive clause. The sentence
    implies that the dog, not a collie, didn't bark.)
8. The dog, which barked, is a collie.
    (Same as number 5 above.)
9. The company hired the men who had gone to college.
    (No comma with a restrictive clause. The sentence
    implies that the company did not hire the men who had
    not gone to college.)
10. The company hired the men, who had gone to college.
    (Same as numbers 5 and 8 above.)

REVIEW OF THE SENTENCE

Before proceeding further, it would be well at this point to review what you have studied so far and to test yourself on past lessons.

■   **A sentence, which expresses a complete thought, consists of a group of two or more related words that forms an independent clause. A sentence may also contain one or more groups of words that form dependent clauses.**

■   **Every sentence begins with a capital letter and ends with a punctuation mark.**

■   **There are four kinds of sentences in regard to use. They are declarative, interrogative, imperative, and exclamatory.**

☐   **Declarative**   — a sentence that makes a statement, that tells something. It ends with a period.

☐   **Interrogative** — a sentence that asks a question. It ends with a question mark.

☐   **Imperative**   — a sentence that asks or tells someone to do something. It ends with a period.

☐   **Exclamatory** — a sentence that expresses strong feeling, such as joy, surprise, sadness, anger. It ends with an exclamation point.

1. Write a declarative sentence and punctuate it correctly.

☐ _____

2. Write an interrogative sentence and punctuate it correctly.

☐ _____

3. Write an imperative sentence and punctuate it correctly.

☐ _____

4. Write an exclamatory sentence and punctuate it correctly.

☐ _____

■   **A sentence is a complete thought expressed in words. The subject is what the sentence (the thought) is about.**

Underline the subject in each of these sentences.

5.   Playing tennis is fun.

6.   The tree stood near the house.

7.   Who will be at the party?

8.   Learning grammar is easy.

9.   The ball rolled into the water.

10.   Honesty is the best policy.

■   **The predicate is what is said about the subject.**

Draw a slanting line to separate the subject from the predicate in each of these sentences.

11.   John won the race.

12.   She has a beautiful voice.

13.   Running in the race was great fun.

14.   Who is coming?

15.   You can do it.

■   **A verb is a necessary part of every sentence. There are two kinds of verbs. One kind shows action; the other shows only a condition or relationship, not any kind of movement or action.**

Underline the verbs in these sentences.

16.   Marie watched the sunset.

17.   She sat in a chair.

18.   The sun shone on Thursday.

19. In the garden the birds sang.
20. After sundown he opened the curtains.

■ **A verb may consist of more than one word.**

Underline the verbs in these sentences.

21. I should have attended class this morning.
22. I could go now.
23. She had been studying her lesson.
24. She will have arrived before noon.
25. I am not going home.

■ **A simple sentence may contain more than one verb.**

Underline the verbs in these simple sentences.

26. Louise ran to the river and looked at the waves.
27. The dog barked and then ran away.
28. I woke early and saw the sunrise.
29. Bill forgot the street name but remembered the house number.
30. Allen wrote a letter and then fell asleep.

■ **A simple sentence may contain two or more subjects.**

Underline the subjects in these sentences.

31. Dave and I volunteered to go.
32. My younger sister and her friend are in Europe this summer.
33. An independent clause and a dependent clause form a complex sentence.
34. Learning computer operation and studying finance are part of the curriculum.
35. Banjos and clarinets are musical instruments.

■ **Two or more sentences written as one form a compound sentence.**

Underline the word that connects the two sentences in each of these compound sentences.

36. I ran fast, but I could not win the race.
37. The grass was wet, so he did not mow it.
38. I looked in the barn, and there I saw the horse.
39. Greg had no money on deposit; therefore, he was unable to write a check.
40. Either Andy will pay the bill, or the company will sue him.

■ **A complex sentence contains an independent clause and one or more dependent clauses.**

Underline the dependent clauses in these complex sentences.

41. Shortly before we arrived, we had a flat tire.
42. I washed my hands before I picked up the vial.
43. Since we returned from Europe, we have remained at home.
44. I joined the Navy when I was only 17 years of age.
45. She is a person who is a joy to visit.

■ **You recall that commas are used to separate nonrestrictive dependent clauses from the rest of the sentence. Also a comma is used to separate a dependent clause from an independent clause in a complex sentence when the dependent clause comes first in the sentence; that is, when it is "out of its natural order."**

Place commas as needed in these complex sentences.

46. The story which I believed was very strange.
47. Although it was raining he continued to work in the garden.
48. The city of Fairbanks which is near the Arctic Circle has very cold winters.

49.   Marie read a book while I washed the dishes.

50.   When she comes in March we will have a celebration.

■   **Two kinds of connectives are used to join simple and complex sentences to form compound or compound-complex sentences. One kind is the coordinating conjunction and the correlating conjunction. A comma is used before a connective of that kind unless there is internal punctuation and then a semicolon is used. Another kind is the conjunctive adverb and the transitional phrase. When either is used to join sentences, a semicolon goes before the connective and generally a comma after it. If no connecting word or words are used, the two sentences must be separated by a semicolon, not a comma.**

The connectives in these compound and compound-complex sentences are in italics.   Punctuate the sentences correctly with commas and semicolons.

51.   The old tree, which had fallen on the lawn that night, was large *so* we hired a man who had a power saw to cut it into firewood.

52.   Since the tree would be used as firewood, he sawed the trunk into short lengths *then* he brought his truck and filled it with branches.

53.   He spoke to me most mornings today he passed by without saying a word.

54.   The Andersons, who are restaurant owners, have been living and working in Atlanta for many years but last Monday, when Mr. Anderson became 70 years of age, they decided to sell their business and retire.

55.   Tom drove the cattle to the pasture where they graze *and* then he returned to the barn.

56.   I fed the dog every evening when it came to the door *otherwise* it would howl and disturb the neighbors.

57.   We were enjoying balmy weather on our vacation in San Juan *at the same time* residents of Buffalo were digging out of snow drifts.

58. We received the news by radio *consequently* we changed our plans.

59. We had planned to return home immediately *instead* we remained in the city for another week.

60. *Either* the weather in Buffalo will improve *or* we will extend our vacation in San Juan.

Now check your answers to see how many you have correct.

ANSWERS

5. Playing tennis
6. The tree
7. Who
8. Learning grammar
9. The ball
10. Honesty

11. John / won the race.
12. She / has a beautiful voice.
13. Running in the race / was great fun.
14. Who / is coming?
15. You / can do it.

16. watched
17. sat
18. shone
19. sang
20. opened
21. should have attended
22. could go
23. had been studying
24. will have arrived
25. am going
26. ran, looked
27. barked, ran
28. woke, saw
29. forgot, remembered
30. wrote, fell

31. Dave and I
32. My younger sister and her friend
33. An independent clause and a dependent clause
34. Learning computer operation and studying finance
35. Banjos and clarinets

36. but
37. so
38. and
39. therefore
40. or

41. Shortly before we arrived
42. before I picked up the vial
43. Since we returned from Europe
44. When I was only 17 years of age
45. who is a joy to visit
46. The story, which I believed, was very strange.
47. Although it was raining, he continued to work in the garden.
48. The city of Fairbanks, which is near the Arctic Circle, has very cold winters.
49. Marie read a book while I washed the dishes.
50. When she comes home in March, we will have a celebration.
51. Place semicolon before the coordinating conjunction *so*.
52. Place semicolon before the conjunctive adverb *then*.
53. Place semicolon after *mornings*; this is a compound sentence that has no conjunction.
54. Place semicolon before coordinating conjunction *but*.
55. Place comma before the coordinating conjunction *and*.
56. Place semicolon before and a comma after the conjunctive adverb *otherwise*.
57. Place a semicolon before and a comma after *at the same time*.
58. Place a semicolon before and a comma after *consequently*.
59. Place a semicolon before and a comma after *instead*.
60. Place a comma before *or*.

2

PARTS OF SPEECH

Sentences are made up of words, and every word is a part of speech when used in a sentence. There are eight parts of speech in the English language. They are: noun (n.), adjective (adj.), pronoun (pron.), preposition (prep.), verb (vb.), conjunction (conj.), adverb (adv.), and interjection (interj.).

When you find a word in the dictionary, you will see that it is followed by an abbreviation in italics indicating what part of speech it is. The abbreviations for parts of speech are shown above in parentheses. You have already been introduced to the verb and the conjunction. In the following lessons, you will learn more about all the parts of speech.

2.1 THE WORD *NOUN* MEANS NAME.

One of the eight parts of speech is the **noun**, a word from the Middle English *nowne* that means *name*. In English grammar, a noun is a name. There are two kinds, *common* and *proper*.

■ **Common nouns apply to all of a kind, such as ocean, city, and man; and they begin with small letters.**

EXAMPLES

The common nouns are in italics.

- ☐ They wanted to go *home*.
- ☐ Walter gave them some *apples*.
- ☐ The *men* swam in the river.
- ☐ New York is a large *city*.
- ☐ Whose *automobile* is that?

■ **Proper nouns name particular persons, places, and things; that is, they name a specific one-of-a-kind; and they always begin with capital letters. For example, there is only one Boston, Massachusetts, or one Atlantic Ocean, so those names are capitalized.**

EXAMPLES

The proper nouns are in italics.

- ☐ Mr. *Smith* came to see us.
- ☐ She read the *New Testament* every day.
- ☐ I have a dog; its name is *Tige*.
- ☐ The *Pirates* play baseball in *Pittsburgh*.
- ☐ He drives a *Buick*.

Among rules of capitalization of proper nouns are these.

■ Capitalize the names of people and titles before names, such as Captain John Smith, and the principal words of titles of books, plays, songs, and poems.

■ Capitalize the days of the week and the months of the year; names of specific buildings, streets and roads, churches, schools, and colleges; of countries and nationalities; of rivers, lakes, islands, and mountains; of cities, states and countries; of clubs, organizations, and athletic teams.

Complete rules for capitalization are given in your English handbook and in the Manual of Style in your dictionary.

FOR PRACTICE

Now test yourself by underlining the common nouns in these sentences.

1. The bridge was closed, so we took the detour.
2. The house was in the third block west of the park.
3. The guests ate dinner on the deck of the boat.
4. I cut the paper with a pair of scissors.
5. The book describes the adventures of a band of pirates.

In these sentences underline the proper nouns that should be capitalized.

6. I am reading spanish literature.
7. The white house in washington is a popular tourist attraction.
8. The first ten amendments to the constitution are called the bill of rights.
9. Farmers in iowa raise great quantities of corn.
10. Yosemite national park is in california.

Now check your answers to see how many you have marked correctly.

ANSWERS

1. bridge, detour
2. house, block, park
3. guests, dinner, deck, boat
4. paper, pair, scissors
5. book, adventures, band, pirates
6. Spanish
7. White House, Washington
8. Constitution, Bill of Rights
9. Iowa
10. Yosemite National Park, California

2.2 NOUNS HAVE NUMBER.

You have learned that a noun is the name of something and that there are common nouns and proper nouns. In writing and printing, a common noun begins with a small letter and a proper noun begins with a capital letter.

■ Nouns also have *number*. A noun may be *singular* number, which means one, or it may be *plural*, which means more than one.

EXAMPLES

□ The word *horse* means one and *horses* means more than one.

One way to change singular to plural in regular nouns is add *s*. Other examples are

□ tree / trees
□ ocean / oceans
□ boat / boats

It really is not that simple, however, because there are many ways of forming the plural of nouns, as explained below. First, note that of the 26 letters in the alphabet of the English language, some are called *vowels*, others are *consonants*. The vowels are *a*, *e*, *i*, *o*, *u*, and sometimes *y*. All the other letters are called consonants. That knowledge can be used in spelling the plurals of nouns that end with the letter *y*.

Rules for forming the plural of nouns.

■ **If the letter of the noun just before the *y* is a vowel, add *s* to make the noun plural.**

EXAMPLES

- □ boy / boys
- □ key / keys
- □ bay / bays

■ **If the letter just before the *y* is a consonant, change the *y* to *i* and add *es*.**

EXAMPLES

- □ army / armies
- □ sky / skies
- □ supply / supplies

There is hardly a rule for forming the plural of nouns that doesn't have exceptions. Words ending with the letter *o* provide examples.

■ **If the letter just before the final *o* of a noun is a vowel, add *s* to form the plural.**

EXAMPLES

- □ zoo / zoos
- □ stereo / stereos

Some exceptions:

- ☐ soprano / sopranos
- ☐ piano / pianos
- ☐ solo / solos

■ **If the letter just before the final *o* is a consonant, add *es* to form the plural.**

- ☐ tomato / tomatoes
- ☐ potato / potatoes
- ☐ hero / heroes

Those two rules for forming the plural of nouns ending with the letter *o* are complicated by the fact that some words ending in *o* may be made plural by adding either *s* or *es*.

- ☐ motto / mottoes or mottos
- ☐ zero / zeros or zeroes
- ☐ mosquito / mosquitoes or mosquitos
- ☐ memento / mementos or mementoes

■ **When two spellings of the plural of a noun are given in the dictionary, the first is preferred but either is correct.**

■ **The inconsistency of rules is shown in the plurals of nouns ending in *f* or *fe*. Some become plural by changing the *f* to *v* and adding *s* or *es*.**

- ☐ knife / knives

- ☐ thief / thieves
- ☐ wife / wives

■ **Other words ending in *f* or *fe*, however, become plural merely by adding *s*.**

- ☐ belief / beliefs
- ☐ proof / proofs

The spelling of plurals is further complicated by the fact that some nouns ending in *f* or *fe* may be spelled either way.

- ☐ scarf / scarves or scarfs
- ☐ hoof / hooves or hoofs

■ **Also note that the plural of nouns ending in *ff* is formed by adding *s*.**

- ☐ tariff / tariffs
- ☐ staff / staffs

■ **Some singular nouns become plural by a change of letters inside the words.**

- ☐ man / men
- ☐ woman / women

- ☐ goose / geese
- ☐ mouse / mice

■ **Some nouns are spelled the same in both the singular and plural form.**

EXAMPLES

- ☐ deer / deer
- ☐ sheep / sheep
- ☐ species / species
- ☐ corps / corps
- ☐ headquarters / headquarters
- ☐ pants / pants
- ☐ scissors / scissors
- ☐ scales / scales

■ **The plural of a compound noun is formed by making the principal word plural.**

EXAMPLES

- ☐ brother-in-law / brothers-in-law
- ☐ by-product / by-products
- ☐ commander-in-chief / commanders-in-chief

■ **Some words from Latin and Greek keep their original spellings in the plural.**

EXAMPLES

- ☐ alga / algae
- ☐ alumnus / alumni
- ☐ datum / data
- ☐ criterion / criteria
- ☐ stimulus / stimuli

The plural of some words from foreign languages, however, are correct with either English or foreign spelling.

- ☐ syllabus / syllabi or syllabuses
- ☐ index / indexes or indices
- ☐ fungus / fungi or funguses
- ☐ formula / formulas or formulae

Because there are so many exceptions to the rules, it is better to memorize spelling than to rely on rules; and when in doubt, use the dictionary. There is no reason for anyone to misspell a word because correct spelling can be found in the dictionary.

■ Nouns have not only number, as explained in this lesson, but they also have *gender* and *case.*

Case is complex, so it will be explained later; but gender is rather simple.

■ Nouns can have one of three genders: *masculine, feminine,* and *neuter.*

Most nouns that denote people and animals are either masculine (male) or feminine (female), such as man/woman, rooster/hen, and buck/doe.

Neuter gender is neither masculine nor feminine; and in the English language, names of inanimate objects, which include most nouns, are neuter gender. The words *day* and *house* are neuter. When we refer to a day or a house, we say *it,* not *he* or *she.* That is, incidentally, in contrast with European languages in which the word *day* is masculine in French *(jour),* in German *(tag),* in Spanish *(dia),* and in Italian *(giorno).* The word *house* is feminine in French *(maison),* in German *(haus),* and in Italian and Spanish *(casa).*

FOR PRACTICE

Write the plural of these nouns in the blanks. If you are not sure of the spelling, use your dictionary.

1.	leaf	_____	2.	brush	_____
3.	baby	_____	4.	fox	_____
5.	fish	_____	6.	latch	_____
7.	oasis	_____	8.	ox	_____
9.	Chinese	_____	10.	knife	_____
11.	athletics	_____	12.	son-in-law	_____
13.	sheriff	_____	14.	fence	_____
15.	child	_____	16.	radius	_____
17.	news	_____	18.	match	_____
19.	sandwich	_____	20.	banjo	_____
21.	dictionary	_____	22.	medium	_____
23.	bill of lading	_____	24.	grotto	_____

Now check your spelling to see how many you have correct.

ANSWERS

1.	leaves	2.	brushes
3.	babies	4.	foxes
5.	fish	6.	latches
7.	oases	8.	oxen
9.	Chinese	10.	knives
11.	athletics	12.	sons-in-law
13.	sheriffs	14.	fences
15.	children	16.	radii or radiuses
17.	news	18.	matches
19.	sandwiches	20.	banjos or banjoes
21.	dictionaries	22.	mediums or media
23.	bills of lading	24.	grottoes or grottos

2.3 PERSONAL PRONOUNS HAVE PERSON, NUMBER, GENDER, AND CASE.

In your study of the parts of speech, you have learned that a *noun* is a name. It is the name of a person, a place, a thing, or an idea.

■ Another part of speech is the *pronoun*, which is a word that stands for a noun, that takes the place of a noun. The prefix *pro* in the word means *for*, so a pronoun is literally *for a noun*. Its use is shown in these sentences.

EXAMPLES

□ *John* gave me some money; *he* is my friend.
In that sentence, the pronoun is *he*; it stands for *John*.

□ *The car* ran into a ditch; *it* was badly damaged.
In that sentence the pronoun is *it*; it stands for *car*.

You already know the words that are called pronouns and often use them, but you may not know how to use them correctly at all times. Many people don't, so it is in using pronouns that they make mistakes. There are eight kinds of pronouns, listed in the next lesson; but the ones in the box on page 72 are those that most often cause difficulty. The reason is that they have *person*, *number*, *gender*, and *case* and change form according to their use in sentences.*

■ Person. The pronouns in the box, except for those on the bottom line, are called *personal pronouns* because they have *person*. Person refers to whether you are speaking of yourself (first person) or of another person or persons (second and third persons). When you speak of yourself only, you use first person singular; that is, you say *I*, *me*, *my*, or *mine*.

---

* The change in form of a word according to its use in the sentence is called *inflection*. An example is *who*, which becomes *whom* in the objective case and *whose* in the possessive case.

PRONOUNS

	Nominative Case	Objective Case	Possessive Case
		Singular Number	
First Person	I	me	my, mine
Second Person	you	you	your, yours
Third Person	he, she, it	him, her, it	his, her, hers, its
		Plural Number	
First Person	we	us	our, ours
Second Person	you	you	your, yours
Third Person	they	them	their, theirs
		Both Singular and Plural	
All Persons	who	whom	whose

EXAMPLES

- □ *I saw* a dog.
- □ The dog came to see *me*.
- □ It is *my* dog.
- □ The dog is *mine*.

When you speak of yourself with others, you use the first person plural pronouns *we*, *us*, *our*, *ours*. When you speak of persons other than yourself, you use second and third person pronouns. See examples in the box.

■ **Number. Personal pronouns have *number*, which means that they are either singular or plural.**

■ **Gender. Some of the personal pronouns have *gender*, which means that they are masculine, feminine, or neuter (male, female or neither male or female).**

■ **Case. *Case* refers to the form a pronoun takes in relationship to other words in the sentence. This is explained in the next chapter.**

FOR PRACTICE

To become better acquainted with these troublesome pronouns, refer to those in the box when you complete these sentences.

Underline the *singular pronouns* in these sentences.

1. They wished her a Merry Christmas.
2. I walked with them to the park.
3. She is a good cook.

Underline the *plural pronouns* in these sentences.

4. We wished her a Merry Christmas.

5. Our house is at the end of the street.
6. Alexander told them about the money.

Underline the *masculine pronoun* in this sentence.

7. They walked with him to the park.

Underline the *feminine pronoun* in this sentence.

8. She is a good cook.

Underline the *pronoun of neuter gender*.

9. Give it to him.

Underline the *first person pronoun* in this sentence.

10. I walked with them to the park.

Underline the *third person pronoun* in this sentence.

11. I walked with them to the park.

Underline the *possessive pronoun* in this sentence.

12. This house is theirs.

Underline the *pronoun in the nominative case* in this sentence.

13. He is a strong man.

Underline the *pronouns in the objective case* in these sentences.

14. I walked with them to the park.
15. You saw whom in the park?

Now check your answers to see how well you have done.

```
┌─────────────────────────────────────────────────────┐
│                    ┌──────────┐                       │
│                    │ ANSWERS  │                       │
│                    └──────────┘                       │
│                                                       │
│   1. her      2. I        3. She    4. We     5. Our  │
│   6. them     7. him      8. She    9. it    10. I    │
│  11. them    12. theirs  13. He    14. them  15. whom │
└─────────────────────────────────────────────────────┘
```

2.4 THERE ARE EIGHT KINDS OF PRONOUNS.

You learned in Lesson 1.11 that relative pronouns (who, which, that, etc.) are used to introduce independent clauses. In Lesson 2.3 you learned that personal pronouns stand for persons and things. Those are two of the eight kinds or classes of pronouns. They are listed here, with examples of their use.

■ *Relative pronouns* **are used to introduce dependent clauses. They are listed in Lesson 1.11.**

EXAMPLES

The relative pronouns are in italics.

□ I caught the horse *that* ran away.
□ That book, *which* is interesting, belongs to George.
□ My uncle, *who* lives in England, has a house for sale.

■ *Personal pronouns*, **which are listed in the box in the previous lesson, stand for persons and things.**

EXAMPLES

□ *He* is *my* uncle.
□ *I* saw *him* yesterday.

■ *Interrogative pronouns* are used to begin or introduce interrogative sentences. They are *who, whom, whose, what, which, that, whoever, whatever,* and *whichever.* Note that they are the same as the relative pronouns, the difference being in their use in the sentence.

EXAMPLES

- □ *Whom* did you ask?
- □ *What* is her name?
- □ *Which* did she ask for?

■ *Demonstrative pronouns* point to or indicate a particular person, thing, or group. They are *this, that, these, those.*

EXAMPLES

- □ *That* is his book.
- □ *This* is an excellent restaurant.

■ *Indefinite pronouns* do not refer to any particular persons or places or things. They are *each, either, neither, any, anyone, one, some, someone, several, others, more, most, none, no one, few, all, everyone, both, everybody, nobody.*

EXAMPLES

- □ *Many* were late for the meeting.
- □ *All* had arrived by 9 o'clock.
- □ *Everyone* had his own automobile.

■ *Reciprocal pronouns* show a mutual relationship. They are *each other* and *one another.*

EXAMPLES

- □ Let us tell *each other* the truth.
- □ We are commanded to love *one another.*

■ *Reflexive pronouns* end with *self* and refer back to the subject. They are *myself, yourself, himself, herself, itself, oneself, themselves, ourselves, yourselves.*

EXAMPLES

☐ They let *themselves* through the gate.
☐ Catherine did *herself* no good.

■ *Intensive pronouns* are the same as reflexive pronouns but emphasize another noun or pronoun in the sentence.

EXAMPLES

☐ She *herself* did all the work.
☐ We did all the work *ourselves.*

Being able to identify all the classes of pronouns is not as important as being able to use pronouns correctly. Their use will be explained in more detail in future lessons. Just now, you should be able to recognize pronouns.

FOR PRACTICE

Underline the pronouns in these sentences.

1. Who came to see Cheryl?
2. Henry Smith, who is a doctor, taught the first aid class.
3. Anyone may play.
4. None of the cans were full.
5. They came promptly.
6. The chair that stands in the corner has a broken leg.
7. Whom did Louise see?

8. Betty swept the floor; she is a good worker.

9. Paul's shirt is blue; mine is white.

10. Sam and Louis have completed their work.

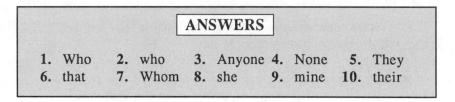

2.5 MOST PRONOUNS HAVE ANTECEDENTS.

You have learned that a pronoun is a word that stands for a noun. In grammar the noun that a pronoun stands for is called the **antecedent**. The word means *that which goes before*.

EXAMPLE

☐ John gave me some money; *he* is my friend.

In that sentence the pronoun *he* stands for *John*. Thus *John* is the antecedent of the pronoun *he*.

EXAMPLES

☐ The *street* was narrow, but *it* was beautiful.
(it / street)
☐ The *man who* lives in the white house is my cousin.
(who / man)
☐ *Mary* and *Helen* had worked hard; *they* were tired.
(they / Mary, Helen)

☐   The *river, which* ran swiftly, was difficult to cross.
(which / river)
☐   *Each* of the boys wanted *his* share of the money.
(his / Each)

To say that a pronoun stands for a noun isn't quite complete. A pronoun may stand for another pronoun, and it may stand for a group of words used as a noun. That a pronoun may stand for another pronoun is shown in the last example above.

EXAMPLE

☐   *Each* of the boys wanted *his* share of the money.

In that sentence the antecedent of the pronoun *his* is *Each*, which is an indefinite pronoun.

Here is an example of a group of words used as a noun.

EXAMPLE

☐   Being dealt a slam hand in bridge, *which* is rare, can present problems in bidding.

The subject of that sentence is *Being dealt a slam hand in bridge*, and that group of words is the antecedent of the relative pronoun *which*. Relative pronouns, you recall, introduce dependent clauses in complex sentences.

Pronouns have three uses.

1.   One use is to ask questions.

EXAMPLES

☐   *Who* is that man?
☐   *What* does he want?

Those are called *interrogative pronouns.*

2. **Another use of pronouns is to introduce or join dependent clauses to independent clauses to form complex sentences.**

EXAMPLES

☐ William, *who* is an excellent pianist, entertained the group.
☐ The house *that* stands on the corner was once my home.

3. **Still another use of pronouns is to avoid the repetition of nouns. It is here that they are used in place of nouns.**

EXAMPLES

☐ James told Martha that *James* was angry at *Martha.*
  (with nouns)
☐ James told Martha that *he was* angry at *her.*
  (with pronouns)

FOR PRACTICE

Underline the antecedents of the pronouns in these sentences. The pronouns are in italics.

1. The chairman *himself* was late for the meeting.
2. Robert told *his* father about the accident.
3. This is the car *that* Oscar bought last week.
4. They amused *themselves* by singing sea chanteys.
5. No one would tell *his* name.
6. The workers were dressed in *their* uniforms.
7. The automobile, *which* was new, ran smoothly.
8. The company watched *its* profits increase rapidly.

9. Caroline said *she* was hungry.

10. This is the house *that* Jack built.

11. *It* is a tale told by an idiot.

12. We wanted *our* team to win.

13. The players believed *they* could win.

14. He won the prize *himself.*

15. This is the woman *who* does our cleaning.

Now check your answers.

ANSWERS

1. chairman	**2.** Robert	**3.** car	**4.** They
5. No one	**6.** workers	**7.** automobile	**8.** company
9. Caroline	**10.** house	**11.** tale	**12.** We
13. players	**14.** He	**15.** woman	

2.6 VERBS HAVE TENSE.

The word *verb* comes from the Latin *verbum* which means *word.* A verb is a part of speech necessary to every sentence because it is not possible to have a complete thought (a complete sentence) without it. In fact, as shown in Lesson 1.2, a sentence may consist of only one word, provided that word is a verb.

EXAMPLES

☐ Stop!
☐ Hurry!

Those are complete sentences with the subject *You* in each understood.

You have already learned that there are two kinds of verbs. One kind shows action; the other shows only a condition or a relationship, not an action.

EXAMPLES

☐ The ball *rolled* down the hill. John *kicked* the ball.
☐ Carol *is* pretty. She *has* a book.

The verbs *rolled* and *kicked* in the first sentences show action. The verbs *is* and *has* in the next sentences do not show action; they show only a condition or a relationship.

You have already learned that a verb may consist of more than one word and that words in front of the main verb are called helping or auxiliary verbs. Each of the verbs in these sentences contains a main verb and one or more helping verbs, with the main verbs and their helpers in italics.

EXAMPLES

☐ I *have been working* in the garden.
☐ They *have been asked* many questions.
☐ Bill *had learned* the lesson.
☐ He *should eat* some food.
☐ When *will* you *go* to London?

By consisting of more than one word, a verb can be more flexible in indicating time. In grammar, verbs are said to have **tense**, which means time of action or condition. Tense is the "when" part of the verb.

■ There are essentially three tenses: present, past, and future. But there are three classes of tenses: simple, perfect, and progressive.

The Simple Tenses

In the simple tenses, the verb is one word except in the future tense and there it always has the helping verb *will* or *shall*.

EXAMPLES

Present tense: ☐ I *know* him.
                        ☐ I *am* hungry.

Past tense: ☐ I *knew* him.
                        ☐ I *was* hungry.

Future tense: ☐ I *will know* him.
                        ☐ I *will be* hungry.

The Perfect Tenses

The perfect tense is used to indicate an action or condition that was or will be completed before another action or condition. Notice that it always has *have* or *had* as a helping verb.

EXAMPLES

Present Perfect: ☐ I *have finished* my work.

Past Perfect: ☐ I *had finished* my work by noon.

Future Perfect: ☐ I *will have finished* my work by noon

The Progressive Tenses

The progressive tense indicates continuing action. The main verb in this tense always ends in *ing*.

EXAMPLES

Present Progressive: ☐ I *am working* hard.

Past Progressive:	☐	I *was working* hard.
Future Progressive:	☐	I *will be working* hard.
Present Perfect Progressive:	☐	I *have been working* hard.
Past Perfect Progressive:	☐	I *had been working* hard.
Future Perfect Progressive:	☐	I *will have been working* hard all day before I complete this job.

FOR PRACTICE

Write in the blank whether the tense of the verb is present, past, or future.

1. She *plays* the piano. _____

2. Sandra *will go* to the store. _____

3. The bird *flew* to a tree. _____

4. He *works* in the garden each morning. _____

5. Louise *is* a happy girl. _____

6. She *will sing* for us. _____

7. He *plays* Dixieland jazz. _____

8. Natalie *will arrive* tomorrow. _____

Write in the blanks whether the verb is simple tense, perfect tense, or progressive tense.

9. The river *is rising* and will overflow its banks soon. _____

10. James got lost in the woods while he *was hunting*. _____

11. He *had arrived* home before nine o'clock. _____

12. He *works* in the garden when he has time. _____

13. Last summer he *visited* in England. _____

14. Mary *will have prepared* supper before sundown. _____

15. I *will go* to work in the morning. _____

16. He *will have worked* twelve hours before he leaves the office this evening. _____

17. Henry *was elected* president of the Club. _____

18. I *have read* all those books. _____

Now check your answers to see if you have all of them identified correctly.

ANSWERS

1. Present	**2.** Future	**3.** Past	**4.** Present
5. Present	**6.** Future	**7.** Present	**8.** Future
9. Progressive	**10.** Progressive	**11.** Perfect	**12.** Simple
13. Simple	**14.** Perfect	**15.** Simple	**16.** Perfect
17. Simple	**18.** Perfect		

2.7 VERBS HAVE FOUR PRINCIPAL PARTS.

Tenses of verbs are derived from the four principal parts: *present tense, present participle, past tense*, and *past participle*. Regular verbs form these parts by adding *ing* for the present participle and *ed, d* or *t* for the past participle. Irregular verbs use *ing* for the present participle but form the past tense and the past participle in different ways.

Present Tense (Base form of verb)	*Present* *Participle*	*Past* *Tense*	*Past* *Participle*

Examples of Regular Verbs

bend	bending	bent	bent
walk	walking	walked	walked
play	playing	played	played
flee	fleeing	fled	fled
compile	compiling	compiled	compiled

Examples of Irregular Verbs

come	coming	came	come
drink	drinking	drank	drunk
fly	flying	flew	flown
go	going	went	gone
lie (to rest)	lying	lay	lain

■   **The present tense may be used as a single word or with such helping verbs as** *do, may, could.*

EXAMPLES

- □ *Drink* the water
- □ Do *write* me a letter.
- □ I *could drink* some water.
- □ I *may write* him a letter.

■   **The past tense is used as a single word with no helping verbs.**

EXAMPLES

- □ I *wrote* to him.
- □ I *sat* on the chair.
- □ I *drank* the water.

Besides the present tense and the past tense, there are participles. The present participle always ends in *ing*. Both the present and the past participial form of the verb always has a helping (an auxiliary) verb.

EXAMPLES

1. *Present Participle*

    □   I *am bending* a wire.
    □   He *was coming* home.
    □   She *is lying* in bed.

2. *Past Participle*

    □   I *had bent* the wire.
    □   They *have come* home.
    □   She *had lain* on the bed for an hour.

It is important to use the correct forms of verbs when speaking or writing, but mistakes are often made because so many verbs in the English language are irregular.

■   *Regular verbs* are those that add *d* or *ed* or *t* for the past tense and the past participle. In other words, the ending is always the same for regular verbs. Examples are given at the top of the list on the page 86.

■   The past tense and the past participle of irregular verbs are formed in various ways, as shown in the examples on page 86, and it is in the use of irregular verbs that most mistakes are made.

If you are not sure whether a verb is regular or irregular, look it up in a good dictionary.* If only the base form (present tense) is listed, the verb is regular. If the verb is irregular, the dictionary will give the past tense and the past participle spellings.

---

* Among those recommended is *Webster's Ninth New Collegiate Dictionary*, published by Merriam-Webster, Inc., Springfield, Mass. A larger recommended dictionary is *The Random House Dictionary of the English Language*, unabridged edition, published by Random House, Inc.

Among irregular verbs that are often misused are *lie*, *lay*, *sit*, and *set*. One reason the verbs *lie* and *lay* are so troublesome is that the word *lay* is the past tense of the verb *lie* and it is also a verb that means to put or place. A chicken can *lay* an egg (put an egg in a nest), but a person does not *lay* in bed. Rather, he or she *lies* (rests) in bed.

Both *lie* and *sit* mean to rest; *lay* and *set* mean to place. The word *lie* also means to tell an untruth; but, although spelled and pronounced the same, it is a different word from *lie* which means to rest.

EXAMPLES

1. *sit* (to rest) — sitting — sat — sat

  □ I *am sitting* on a chair.
  □ I *have sat* on that chair.
  □ *Sit* on that chair.
  □ The hen *is sitting* on the nest.

2. *set* (to place or put) — setting — set — set

  □ *Set* the vase on the shelf.
  □ We *set* the table this morning.
  □ Has the table been *set*?
  □ *Set* the hen on the nest.

3. *lie* (to rest) — lying — lay — lain

  □ The book *lies* (rests) on the table.
  □ The book *is lying* (resting) on the table.
  □ The book *lay* (rested) on the table.
  □ The book *has lain* (has rested) on the table for a week.

4. *lay* (to place or put) — laying — laid — laid

  □ He *lays* (places) the book on the table.
  □ He *laid* (placed) the book on the table.
  □ He *has laid* (has placed) the book on the table.

5. *lie* (to be untruthful) — lying — lied — lied

  □ He *lies*.
  □ He *is lying*.

☐   He *lied*.
☐   He *has lied* often.

FOR PRACTICE

Underline the correct verb in each sentence.

1.   She is (setting, sitting) on a cushion.

2.   He (lay, laid) on the bed.

3.   The woman is (laying, lying) on the bed.

4.   Sally has (laid, lain) in bed all day.

5.   She (set, sat) the table for dinner.

6.   (Set, sit) the hen on the nest.

7.   He (had gone, had went) to the store.

8.   He (had sang, had sung) the song many times.

9.   The bird (drowned, drownded) in the pool.

10.   She (did, done) it.

11.   We (hung, hanged) the picture in the hallway.

12.   He (set, sat) in a chair all day.

13.   She (has drunk, has drank) all the lemonade.

14.   I have (wrote, written) him a letter.

15.   The boat has (sank, sunk) near the bank of the river.

ANSWERS			
1. sitting	2. lay	3. lying	4. lain
5. set	6. Set	7. had gone	8. had sung
9. drowned	10. did	11. hung	12. sat
13. has drunk	14. written	15. sunk	

2.8 VERBS ALSO HAVE VOICE AND MOOD.

In your study of grammar, you should learn these two properties of verbs, *voice* and *mood*.

■ *Voice* pertains only to action verbs, and such verbs may be in active or passive voice.

■ A verb is in *active voice* when the subject acts upon the object.

EXAMPLE

☐ Mark kicked the ball.
In that sentence the subject, Mark, acted upon the object, the ball, by kicking it.

■ A verb is in *passive voice* when the verb makes its subject represent the receiver of an act.

EXAMPLE

☐ The ball was kicked by Mark.
In that sentence the subject, the ball, received the action.

EXAMPLES

Active voice:	☐ John shot a bear.
Passive voice:	☐ A bear was shot by John.
Active voice:	☐ Mary wore a blue dress.
Passive voice:	☐ A blue dress was worn by Mary.

The use of active and passive voice will be discussed later in the chapter on "Building Better Sentences."

■ *Mood*, which was formerly called mode, pertains to the kind of thought expressed in a sentence. There are three moods: *indicative, imperative, subjunctive.*

■ A verb is in the *indicative mood* when it is used in a sentence that makes a statement or asks a question. In Lesson 1.1 these are called declarative and interrogative sentences.

EXAMPLES

- □ She goes to the market every Tuesday morning.
- □ Does she go to the market every Tuesday morning?

■ A verb is in the *imperative mood* when the sentence gives a command.

EXAMPLES

- □ *Go* to the market.
- □ *Buy* some vegetables.

You learned previously that only the base form (present tense) of the verb is used in imperative sentences and the subject of those sentences is *You* understood.

EXAMPLES

- □ (You) *Go* to the market.
- □ (You) *Buy* some vegetables.

Being able to recognize the indicative and the imperative moods of verbs is not very important in everyday life, but knowing how to use the subjunctive mood correctly may be useful. However, Fowler and Fowler in their authoritative book, *The King's English*, published more than half a century ago, state that the subjunctive "is almost meaningless to Englishmen, the thing having so nearly perished." Still, to make your study of grammar more complete, you should have at least a passing acquaintance with the subjunctive mood.

■   The *subjunctive mood* is used in expressing a wish or regret and in stating a condition that does not exist or is not true or is a necessity.

EXAMPLES

A wish: □ I wish I *were* a magician.
A condition
contrary to fact: □ If I *were* a magician, I would surprise you.
A necessity: □ It is important that he *answer* the letter
                      today.

Note how the subjunctive differs.

Subjunctive: □ If he *be* king, let him proclaim it.
Imperative: □ If he *is* king, let him proclaim it.

Subjunctive: □ I wish I *were* hungry enough to eat that
                      cake.
Indicative: □ I wish I *was* hungry enough to eat that
                      cake.

Also note that the subjunctive mood is always used in dependent clauses, not in independent clauses.

EXAMPLES

The dependent clauses are in italics.

□ *Even if he were honest*, I wouldn't vote for him.
□ I could play tennis better *if I were younger*.

And note the use of *were* instead of *was* whether the subject is singular or plural.

EXAMPLES

Singular subject: □ I wish I *were* safely home.
Plural subject: □ I wish they *were* safely home.

The same form is used in the present subjunctive of other verbs, whether the subject is singular or plural.

EXAMPLES

□ It is necessary that he *call* me today.
□ It is necessary that they *call* me today.

□ We desire that he *take* his medicine now.
□ We desire that they *take* their medicine now.

It is common to hear someone say, "If it was *me*..." or "If it were *me*...," but standard English requires the use of *I* rather than *me*, "If it were *I*...."

The expressions of "If it *was me*..." in the indicative mood and "If it *were me*..." in the subjunctive mood are called *colloquial*.

Colloquial refers to the language that many, perhaps most, people use in familiar and informal conversation. For example, you ask, "Who is it?" The reply, "It's me," is colloquial because in standard English the reply would be, "It is I." Colloquial language is acceptable in informal conversation, but not in writing.

EXAMPLES

Colloquial language: □ If it were *me* who had to make the choice, I would buy common stock rather than bonds.

Standard English: □ If it were *I* who had to make the choice, I would buy common stock rather than bonds.

One cannot say that the expressions "It's me" and "If it were *me*" are wrong because there really is no right or wrong in English grammar. No official institute or organization establishes rules for grammar and usage in the English language as does the Academie Francaise for French. Rather, rules for standard English are determined largely by consensus, by tradition, and by the works of recognized writers.

Language is constantly undergoing gradual change, with the result that new words are added, the meaning of old words change, some words fall into disuse, and some words and expressions once considered colloquial become accepted as standard.

FOR PRACTICE

If by now you have a fair understanding of the mood of verbs, test yourself in this manner: Each of these five sentences contains a verb in the subjunctive mood. In the blanks, write the indicative or imperative form of each verb.

EXAMPLE

☐   He treats me as if I *were* a mental cripple. _____am_____

1. Although he *be* president, he cannot do that. _____
2. Unless he *come*, we will be lost. _____
3. If this money *were* real, we could spend it. _____
4. Our hope is that she *cook* the dinner. _____
5. We request that John *go* there soon. _____

Now reverse it. The verbs in these sentences are in the indicative mood. Write the subjunctive form for each in the blanks.

6. If this money *was* real, we could spend it. _____
7. If this money *is* counterfeit, we could be arrested. _____

8. Even though he *apologizes*, I will never
   forgive him.   _____

9. We wish that she *receives* special care.   _____

10. Be it resolved that the Committee *approves*
    the report as submitted.   _____

Then check yourself on active and passive voice. Rewrite these
five sentences so that they are in passive voice.

11. She blew out the candle.

    □ _____

12. Louise paid the man the money.

    □ _____

13. Henry wrote a letter to his sister.

    □ _____

14. A bee stung the boy.

    □ _____

15. Hundreds of people attended the ball game.

    □ _____

Now rewrite these sentences so that they are in active voice.

16. The classes were taught by older women.

    □ _____

17. The church bell was rung by the sexton.

    □ _____

18. The packages were carried to the post office by Henry.

    □ _____

19. The names were listed on the ledger by the clerk.

    □ _____

20. The green dress was worn by my sister.

    □ _____

ANSWERS

1. is   2. comes   3. was   4. cooks
5. goes   6. were   7. be or were 8. apologize
9. receive 10. approve
11. The candle was blown out by her.
12. The man was paid the money by Louise.
13. A letter to his sister was written by Henry.
14. The boy was stung by a bee.
15. The ball game was attended by hundreds of people.
16. Older women taught the classes.
17. The sexton rang the church bell.
18. Henry carried the packages to the post office.
19. The clerk listed the names on the ledger.
20. My sister wore the green dress.

2.9 THERE ARE THREE KINDS OF PREDICATE COMPLEMENTS.

As you have learned, a sentence may consist of only two words, a subject and a verb, and sometimes the subject is implied.

EXAMPLES

☐ He stopped.
☐ She laughed.
☐ Harry smiled.
☐ Hurry! (*You* is implied.)

In each of these sentences, the verb is the entire predicate. There are some sentences, however, that would be incomplete with only a subject and a verb.

- ☐ He felt...
- ☐ It smells...
- ☐ Louise was...
- ☐ Michael hit...

Something is needed in the predicate in addition to the verb to make each of those sentences complete. In grammar, the word or words that complete such sentences are called **predicate complements**. A *complement** is something that completes or makes perfect.

■ **There are three kinds of predicate complements. One kind describes the subject and is called a *predicate adjective*.**

EXAMPLES

- ☐ She looked *old*.
- ☐ Mary is *pretty*.
- ☐ This drink tastes *bitter*.

■ **Another kind is called a *predicate nominative* and it refers back to the subject. In one sense, it renames the subject.**

EXAMPLES

- ☐ It was *she*.   (It   she)
- ☐ Who are *they*?   (Who   they)
- ☐ George is a *cook*. (George   cook)

■ **Still another kind of predicate complement is the *object complement*, but in this book it is called *the object of the verb*. In a sentence of this kind, the verb is always an action verb and the object is the person or thing that receives the action of the verb.**

---

* The word must not be confused with the word *compliment*, which is an expression of praise or esteem.

EXAMPLES

- ☐ Dave kicked *the ball*.
- ☐ She ate *the candy*.
- ☐ He scored *a goal*.

Being able to recognize predicates and predicate complements is important in the study of grammar. First, remember that some sentences are complete without predicate complements.

EXAMPLES

- ☐ She laughed *loudly*.
- ☐ John stopped *laughing*.
- ☐ The cat jumped to *the table*.

Each of those sentences would be complete without the words in italics in the predicate. The words in italics add information, but they are not essential to complete the thoughts, not necessary to make the sentences complete.

The predicates of many sentences, however, require complements to make the sentences complete. As stated before, there are three kinds of predicate complements.

1.   *The predicate adjective* describes the subject. Note how the words in italics in these sentences tell something about the subject.

EXAMPLES

- ☐ The clouds were *dark and threatening*.
- ☐ John appeared *idle all afternoon*.
- ☐ She became *ill after supper*.
- ☐ The meat seemed *rancid*.
- ☐ This book is *exciting*.

The verbs used in those sentences are called *linking verbs* because they link the subject to the predicate adjective.

2. *The predicate nominative* is a noun or pronoun (him, her, they, John, teacher, merchant, etc.) that in a sense renames the subject.

EXAMPLES

- [ ] This book is a *classic*.
- [ ] She became a *lawyer*.
- [ ] Was it *she*?
- [ ] It is *he*.
- [ ] Ricardo is a *student*.

3. *The object complement*, or *object of the verb*, is the person or thing that receives the action of the verb.

EXAMPLES

The objects of the verbs are in italics.

- [ ] The book tells *an exciting story*.
- [ ] The drillers struck *oil*.
- [ ] *Whom* shall we nominate?
- [ ] James kissed *the girl* on the cheek.
- [ ] The child drank *a glass of milk*.

FOR PRACTICE

Write letters in the blanks to indicate whether the complement in italics is A — a predicate adjective, or N — a predicate nominative, or O — the object of the verb. There are five of each.

1. She is *an entertainer*. _____

2. She entertained *the audience*. _____

3. The attendant washed *the windshield*. _____

4. The stamps were *worthless*. _____

5. The food tasted *good*.   _____

6. Henry is *the coach*.   _____

7. The cadets chose *a leader*.   _____

8. The girl was *our choice* for queen.   _____

9. He looked *unhappy*.   _____

10. It is *she*.   _____

11. He drove *the car* carefully.   _____

12. He is *an attorney* in Springfield.   _____

13. I feel *miserable*.   _____

14. The smiling girl cut *the birthday cake*.   _____

15. Richard seemed *nervous*.   _____

Now check your answers.

ANSWERS

1. N	2. O	3. O	4. A	5. A
6. N	7. O	8. N	9. A	10. N
11. O	12. N	13. A	14. O	15. A

2.10 A TRANSITIVE VERB REQUIRES AN OBJECT.

You have learned that some verbs require predicate complements to complete their meaning and that there are three kinds of predicate complements. They are *predicate adjective*, *predicate nominative*, and *object complement* which in this book is called *the object of the verb*.

■ Verbs themselves are classified as *transitive* or *intransitive*, depending upon whether an object is necessary to complete the meaning. A verb is said to be transitive when it shows action on a person, place, or thing. Stated another way, a transitive verb requires an object to complete its meaning.

EXAMPLES

☐   Carlos kicked the ball.

In that sentence *the ball* received the action of the verb *kicked*. The verb is transitive because it has an object that received its action. Here are more sentences that have transitive verbs, with the direct objects (receivers of the action of the verbs) in italics.

☐   Marcus loves *his work*.
☐   I play *the piano*.
☐   He befriended *me*.
☐   You saw *him*.

■   Verbs that do not require objects to complete their meaning are called *intransitive verbs*. They may have complements, and they may or may not show action; but they don't show action on the object. All the verbs in the sentences below are intransitive.

EXAMPLES

Action Verbs/No Objects

☐   He *went* to the store.
☐   She *smiled*.
☐   He *waited* for two hours.

Linking Verbs/No Objects

☐   He *is* my friend.
☐   John *had been* a teacher.
☐   Janet *seemed* happy.

■   The difference between transitive and intransitive verbs is that transitive verbs take and have direct objects, intransitive verbs do not.

Some verbs are always transitive and require objects to complete their meaning; some are always intransitive but may require a complement to complete their meaning; and some verbs may be either transitive or intransitive, depending on how they are used in sentences.

When you think about it, you realize that some verbs just can't have objects. You can *hit* a ball, but you can't *look* a ball, or *look* anything else. You can *look* at something, but that does not show any action on the object looked at. You can *see* an object, but you can't *go* anything. So such verbs as *look* and *go* are examples of verbs that are always intransitive.

Here are examples of verbs that may be either transitive or intransitive, depending on their use.

| EXAMPLES |

Transitive Verbs	Intransitive Verbs
☐ She *plays* the piano.	☐ The child *plays* in the park.
☐ She *sang* a beautiful song.	☐ She *sings* beautifully.
☐ He *read* a book.	☐ He *reads* well.

You can find out whether a verb is transitive, intransitive, or may be used either way in your dictionary. If a word is a verb, it will be followed by the italic letters *vb*. A transitive verb is marked by the italic letters *vt* and an intransitive verb by the italic letters *vi*.

FOR PRACTICE

If the verb is transitive (has a direct object), write T in the blank. If the verb is intransitive, write I in the blank. There are five of each.

1. I *like* ice cream. _____

2. Ice cream *tastes* good. _____

3. Gloria *was* angry. _____

4. She *is* a pretty girl. _____

5. The committee *elected* a chairman. _____

6. He *closed* the door. _____

7. That *seems* strange. _____

8. Who *is* he?   ———————

9. Our team *won* the game.   ———————

10. Frank *threw* the towel to me.   ———————

ANSWERS				
1. T	**2.** I	**3.** I	**4.** I	**5.** T
6. T	**7.** I	**8.** I	**9.** T	**10.** T

2.11 AN INTRANSITIVE VERB HAS NO OBJECT.

In the previous lesson you learned that a transitive verb requires a direct object to complete its meaning. The object is the receiver of the action of the verb and is thus called the object complement, or object of the verb, or direct object.

Intransitive verbs may require complements to complete their meaning, but those complements are not receivers of the action of the verbs. Rather as you learned in Lesson 2.9, an intransitive verb links the subject of the sentence to a predicate complement that either renames the subject (*John* is my *father*) or describes the subject in some manner (*He* is *tall*).

One of the most commonly used verbs in the English language that shows no action is the verb *be*. Forms of that verb include *am*, *is*, *was*, *were*, *shall be*, *have been*, *had been*, and so forth. All forms of the verb *be* are called linking verbs because they link the predicate complement to the subject of the sentence.

The predicate complement may describe the subject, in which case it is called a **predicate adjective**.

EXAMPLES

□ This cake is *good*.
□ She was *successful*.

Or the predicate complement may be a noun or a pronoun that renames the subject, in which case it is called a **predicate nominative**.

EXAMPLES

☐ She is *my sister*.
☐ Eric will be a *hero*.
☐ It was *she*.

The verbs in those sentences are forms of the verb *be* and are *linking verbs*. They link the subject to the predicate but do not indicate any action on the predicate. Besides forms of the verb *be*, such as *is*, *was*, *were*, a number of other verbs can serve as linking verbs. The most common are these:

appear	look	seem
believe	prove	smell
become	remain	sound
feel	turn	taste
grow	stay	

EXAMPLES

☐ The room *seems* empty.
☐ Nancy *looked* unhappy.
☐ The apple *tastes* sweet.

FOR PRACTICE

The sentences below contain intransitive verbs followed by predicate complements. The verbs are in italics. If the predicate complement is a predicate adjective (that is, if it describes the subject), write PA in the blank. If the predicate complement is a predicate nominative (that is, it renames the subject), write PN in the blank.

1. The actor *appears* tired.   _____

2. John *became* a farmer.   _____

3. It *was* the early morning train.   _____

4. Richard *is* an excellent teacher.   _____

5. Who *is* it?   _____

6. She *is* my little sister.   _____

7. The rose *looks* beautiful.   _____

8. The program *was* enjoyable.   _____

9. William *is* studious.   _____

10. He *remained* an officer all year.   _____

ANSWERS				
1. PA	2. PN	3. PN	4. PN	5. PN
6. PN	7. PA	8. PA	9. PA	10. PN

2.12 ADJECTIVES MODIFY NOUNS AND PRONOUNS.

So far in your study of grammar you have learned about four of the eight parts of speech: nouns, pronouns, verbs, and conjunctions.

Another part of speech is the **adjective**. The word adjective (*ad jective*) means something added to something else. If you write *a man*, and then you write *a tall man*, you have added to the meaning of the noun *man*. The word you have added is called an *adjective*.

■ **An *adjective* is a word that describes a noun or a pronoun. In grammar, an adjective is said to *modify* a noun or a pronoun.**

EXAMPLES

| pretty | tall | happy |
| good | sweet | red |

In addition to such adjectives as those above, many kinds of words are used as adjectives:

EXAMPLES

Proper Names:	☐	*Spanish* Language
Possessive Pronouns:	☐	*my* book / *their* house
Interrogative Pronouns:	☐	*Which* book is mine?
Demonstrative Adjectives:	☐	*this* book / *that* house
Numbers:	☐	*two* kittens / *four* men
Colors:	☐	*blue* ribbon / *yellow* rose

■ **Two or more words may be written to form a compound adjective; and when that is done, it should be joined by a hyphen.***

EXAMPLES

- ☐ an all-American boy
- ☐ a five-day festival
- ☐ a fifty-cent cup of coffee
- ☐ hand-to-hand combat

---

* Proper use of the hyphen helps the reader and often affects the meaning. As examples, ten dollar-bills is not the same as ten-dollar bills and four day-trips is not the same as four-day trips.

If you don't know whether to use a hyphen when writing a compund word, consult your dictionary. There you will find syllables separated by small dots, a hyphen indicated by a small dash, and some compound words written as separate words with a space between them. Examples: láw·ful (solid word), law-abiding (hyphenated word), and lawn tennis (two words).

■ Compound adjectives come before the nouns or pronouns they modify. Hyphens are not used when the same modifiers are predicate adjectives.

EXAMPLES

Before the noun: □   a four-year-old girl
Predicate adjective: □   The girl was four years old.

■ Hyphens are not generally used when proper names such as New Zealand mountains and New York subway are used as adjectives. A hyphen should be used, however, in such constructions as German-American Club or Anglo-Spanish Alliance, where two separate adjectives are combined.

■ A hyphen is not generally used when the first word of the modifiers ends in *ly*.

EXAMPLE

□   *Highly seasoned food*

■ A series of adjectives is punctuated with commas while a compound adjective is punctuated with hyphens.

EXAMPLES

Series: □   It was a long, blue, beautiful lagoon.
Compound: □   She had up-to-date information.

In your study of predicate complements, you learned that a predicate complement modifies or describes the subject of the sentence, either by renaming the subject (a predicate complement) or by describing the subject (a predicate adjective). In both cases adjectives may be used as shown in these examples of predicate nominatives and predicate adjectives, where the adjectives are in italics.

EXAMPLES

☐ He was a *good* boy.
(The predicate nominative *boy* is described by the adjective *good*.)

☐ The candy is *sweet*.
(The predicate adjective *sweet* describes the subject *candy*.)

☐ It was a *long* road.
(The predicate nominative *road* is described by the adjective *long*.)

☐ Mary was an *unhappy* girl.
(The predicate nominative *girl* is described by the adjective *unhappy*.)

FOR PRACTICE

Underline the adjective in each of these sentences.

1. I saw five ducks on the lake.
2. He was the tallest man in the room.
3. This is the best kind of apple.
4. He drove an Italian car.
5. There was a sudden change in the weather.

Punctuate the compound adjectives with hyphens in these sentences as needed.

6. We visited three South American countries.
7. He was an employee of the Southern Pacific Railroad.
8. Chairman elect Smith presided.
9. The police made a house to house search.
10. John competed in the 100 yard dash.

11. The candidate won by a two thirds' majority.

12. He was given well deserved applause.

13. At my college the coach player relationship was excellent.

14. The man was injured in a head on crash.

15. His son in law was an attorney.

Now check your answers.

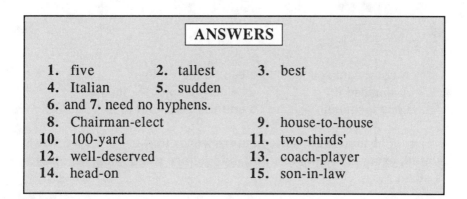

ANSWERS

1. five   2. tallest   3. best
4. Italian   5. sudden
6. and 7. need no hyphens.
8. Chairman-elect   9. house-to-house
10. 100-yard   11. two-thirds'
12. well-deserved   13. coach-player
14. head-on   15. son-in-law

2.13 THE ARTICLES ARE *A*, *AN*, AND *THE*.

Three of the most commonly used words in the English language are *a*, *an*, and *the*. In grammar those three words are called **articles**; and before nouns, where they are generally used, they are classified as adjectives.

EXAMPLES

☐ *a* computer
☐ *an* apple
☐ *the* man

■ The word *the* is a *definite article* because it indicates a definite place, person, or thing. The words *a* and *an* are called *indefinite articles* because they do not indicate anything specific.

When you say *the car*, you are speaking of a particular or specific car; but *a car* or *an apple* could be one among many.

■ The article *a* is used before words that begin with a consonant sound and before words that begin with a sounded *h* and with a long *u* sound.

EXAMPLES

A consonant sound: □ a cup / a log / a fig
A sounded *h*: □ a helper / a hotel / a hundred
Long *u* sound: □ a uniform / a useful tool

■ The article *an* is used before words that begin with a vowel sound, except the long *u* sound, and before words that begin with a silent *h*.

You recall that the vowels are *a*, *e*, *i*, *o*, *u*, and sometime *y*. All other letters are consonants.*

EXAMPLES

A vowel sound: □ an Indian / an action / an ostrich
A silent *h*: □ an hour / an heiress / an herb
A short *u* sound: □ an unhealthful / an understatement

Note that the article *a* is used before *hundred* and *an* before the word *hour*. The word *hundred* begins with a consonant sound, *h*; but the letter *h* is silent in the word *hour*, so the beginning sound of hour is that of a vowel.

---

* When *a* and *an* are used correctly before vowels and consonants, you will find it easier to say, for instance, "Call me in *an* hour" than to say, "Call me in *a* hour."

The use of articles makes a difference in meaning.

■   **The rule is that the article should be repeated when separate objects are referred to.**

EXAMPLES

☐   On the farm was a barn and shed.   (one building)
☐   On the farm were a barn and a shed.   (two buildings)

☐   In the office we were introduced to the secretary and treasurer.   (one person)
☐   In the office we were introduced to the secretary and the treasurer.   (two persons)

Use of the articles *a* and *an* with *kind of* and *sort of* is considered incorrect.

EXAMPLES

Correct: ☐   What kind of dog is it?
              ☐   What sort of book is it?
Incorrect: ☐   What kind of a dog is it?
              ☐   What sort of a book is it?

Correct: ☐   What sort of argument is that?
              ☐   What sort of man was he?
Incorrect: ☐   What sort of an argument is that?
              ☐   What sort of a man was he?

FOR PRACTICE

Underline the correct article in each of these sentences.

1.   A reference book should have (a, an) index.
2.   He considered the award (a, an) honor.

3. It was (a, an) unique idea.

4. He placed the letter in (a, an) envelope.

5. That stray dog needs (a, an) owner.

6. Sally needs (a, an) helper.

Now check your answers.

ANSWERS

1. an index   2. an honor   3. a unique idea
4. an envelope   5. an owner   6. a helper

2.14   AN ADVERB IS A MODIFIER.

The **adverb** is another part of speech. (ad + verb = add to verb).
An adverb is a word that modifies (describes) a verb, an adjective, or
another adverb. That is not as difficult to understand as it sounds.
These sentences show how adverbs are used.

EXAMPLES

☐ Cheryl sang *beautifully*.   (adverb)
☐ Cheryl is *beautiful*   (adjective)

If the first sentence, the verb *sang* tells what Cheryl did. The
adverb *beautifully* tells how she did it. The word *beautifully* is an
adverb that modifies the verb *sang*.

The word *beautiful* in the second sentence is an adjective because
it describes (modifies) the noun *Cheryl*; and you remember from your
previous lesson that an adjective is a word that describes or modifies a
noun or pronoun.

EXAMPLE

☐   He is an exceedingly skillful carpenter.

In that sentence, the word *skillful* is an adjective. It modifies the noun *carpenter*. But the word *exceedingly* is an adverb; it modifies the adjective *skillful* by telling how skillful the carpenter is.

EXAMPLE

☐   The carpenter works very fast.

In that sentence, the word *fast* is an adverb. It modifies the verb by telling how the carpenter works. The word *very* is also an adverb; it modifies the adverb *fast* by telling how he works.

Here are two more sentences that contain adverbs that modify adverbs.

EXAMPLES

☐   I walked *more* slowly than Brenda.
☐   She talked *so* softly that I could barely hear her.

The adverbs *slowly* and *softly* modify the verbs *walked* and *talked* in those sentences. The adverbs *more* and *so* modify the adverbs *slowly* and *softly*.

FOR PRACTICE

Underline the adverbs in these sentences.

1. They lived happily.
2. Can she play the piano well?
3. I often think of her.

4. He spoke slowly.

5. Janet laughed loudly.

6. I waited patiently for him to speak.

7. He scored poorly on the test.

8. We are in reasonably good health.

9. She spoke the language perfectly.

In these sentences the adverbs are in italics. Underline the word in each sentence that the adverb modifies.

10. The horses broke *evenly* from the starting gate.

11. We should hear from him *soon*.

12. The airplane flew so *fast* that it was soon out of sight.

13. The music was played *softly*.

14. He stood *motionless* in the darkness.

15. *Slowly* he began to arrange the flowers.

16. The girl *only* smiled but did not speak.

17. The shelves were *completely* bare.

18. We thought he managed the team *well*.

19. Olivia walked *carefully* across the busy highway.

Now check your answers to see how many you have right.

ANSWERS			
1. happily	2. well	3. often	4. slowly
5. loudly	6. patiently	7. poorly	8. reasonably
9. perfectly	10. broke	11. hear	12. flew
13. was played	14. stood	15. began	16. smiled
17. bare	18. managed	19. walked	

2.15 ADJECTIVES AND ADVERBS ARE DIFFERENT.

An adverb should be placed as closely as possible to the word it modifies. The reason is that the placement affects the meaning. That is shown by the placement of the word *only* in these sentences.

EXAMPLES

    □ Only I love you.
    □ I love only you.

The first sentence means that *you* are loved by only one person and that person is I. The second sentence means that you are the only one I love (but it is possible that others love you, too).

■ **To use correct grammar, you must be able to distinguish between adjectives and adverbs. Adjectives add to the meaning of nouns and pronouns. Adverbs add to the meaning of verbs, adjectives, and other adverbs.**

EXAMPLES

    □ The discussion was *brief*.
       (*Brief* is an adjective that describes the noun *discussion*.)

    □ He discussed the subject *briefly*.
       (*Briefly* is an adverb that modifies the verb *discussed*; it tells how the subject was discussed.)

    □ He spoke in a *loud* voice.
       (*Loud* is an adjective that modifies the noun *voice*.)

    □ He spoke *loudly*.
       (*Loudly* is an adverb that modifies the verb *spoke* by telling how he spoke.)

    □ He spoke in a *very* loud voice.
       (*Very* is an adverb that modifies the adjective *loud* by telling how he spoke.)

☐ His performance on the examination was *bad*.
(*Bad* is an adjective that modifies the noun *performance*.)

☐ He did *poorly* on the examination.
(*Poorly* is an adverb that modifies the verb *did*; it tells how he did.)

☐ He did *very* poorly on the examination.
(*Very* is an adverb that modifies the adverb *poorly*; it tells how poorly he did.)

■ **Adverbs tell *when*, *where*, *how*, and *how much* in relation to the verb.**

EXAMPLES

☐ He arrived *yesterday*.
(The adverb *yesterday* tells *when* he arrived.)

☐ He drove *north*.
(The adverb *north* tells *where* he drove.)

☐ He drove slowly.
(The adverb *slowly* tells *how* he drove.)

☐ The car was completely rebuilt.
(The adverb *completely* tell *how much* the car was rebuilt.)

■ **A common error is using an adverb as an adjective and an adjective as an adverb. Remember that adjectives modify nouns and pronouns; adverbs modify verbs, adjectives, and other adverbs.**

EXAMPLES

Correct: ☐ They ran *evenly* for a short distance.
(The adverb *evenly* modifies the verb *ran*.)
Incorrect: ☐ They ran *even* for a short distance.
(The adjective *even* cannot modify the verb *ran*.)

Correct: □   He was lying *comfortably* on the couch.
                    (The adverb *comfortably* modifies the verb *lying*.)

Incorrect: □   He was lying *comfortable* on the couch.
                    (The adjective *comfortable* cannot modify the verb *lying*.)

Correct   □   She looked *contentedly* at the dress.
                    (The adverb *contentedly* modifies the verb *looked*.)

Incorrect: □   She looked *contented* at the dress.
                    (The adjective *contented* cannot modify the verb *looked*.)

To avoid errors, it is necessary to distinguish between adjectives and adverbs and to determine what is being modified in the sentence. Doing so, however, is not always simple, for these reasons.

■   **Most adverbs end in *ly*, but not all. Some adjectives also end in *ly*.**

EXAMPLES

□   He heard an *unearthly* noise.
    (*Unearthly* is an adjective that modifies the noun *noise*.)

□   He saw a *ghostly* figure.
    (*Ghostly* is an adjective that modifies the noun *figure*.)

Among other adjectives that end in *ly* are *daily* bread, *early* dawn, *elderly* man, *friendly* dog, *lively* kitten, *lonely* widow, *lovely* rose.

■   **Some words have the same form whether they are used as adjectives or adverbs.**

EXAMPLES

Adverb: □   He drove so *fast* that he won the race.
Adjective: □   He drove a *fast* car.

■   The rule is that adverbs modify verbs, adjectives, and other adverbs; adjectives modify nouns and pronouns. It is therefore incorrect to use an adverb to modify a noun or a pronoun, or to use an adjective to modify a verb. Errors of this kind frequently occur in the use of the words *real, good, bad, well,* and *slow.*

You may hear someone say, "He played real bad," and you know what that person means; but what he said is not considered standard English.

EXAMPLES

☐ This is a *real* diamond.   (Correct as an adjective)
☐ He played *really* well today.   (Correct as an adverb)

One common failure to distinguish between adverbs and adjectives occurs in the use of the adjective *good* instead of the adverb *well.* Here the meanings of the words differ. The word *good* means, among other things, well behaved or of favorable character. To say that a person *plays good* really means that he behaves properly while playing. The word *bad* is the opposite; to say that a person played *bad* means that he misbehaved while playing. If he played *well*, he played skillfully.

EXAMPLES

☐ He played *well*.   (Correct)
☐ He played *good*.   (Incorrect)

Both words in italics in those two sentences are used to modify the verb *played.* The word *well* is properly used as an adverb, but *good* is an adjective and should not be used to modify a verb.

EXAMPLES

Correct: ☐ She hears *well* with her new hearing aid.
Incorrect: ☐ She hears *good* with her new hearing aid.

Correct: □   He is a *good* man.
Correct: □   This food tastes *good*.

In the sentence, He is a good man, the word *good* is an adjective modifying *man*. In the sentence, This food tastes good, the word *good* is a predicate adjective modifying *food*. You learned about predicate adjectives in Lesson 2.9.

Although the word *good* is an adjective, and in standard English is not used as an adverb, the word *well* can be used as an adverb or as an adjective, depending on its use in the sentence. It may be used as as adjective to add meaning to a noun or pronoun or as an adverb to add meaning to a verb, an adjective, or another adverb.

EXAMPLES

Adverb: □   He feels *well*.
                        (*well* modifies the verb *feels*)
Adjective: □   He is a *well* man.
                        (*well* modifies the noun *man*)
Predicate adjective: □   He is *well*.
                        (*well* modifies the pronoun *He*)

The word *bad* is an adjective; *badly* is an adverb.

EXAMPLES

Adverb: □   He played *badly*.
                    □   He was *badly* hurt.

Adjective: □   He is a *bad* man.
                    □   This food is *bad*.

The expressions *look bad*, *feel bad*, *smell bad*, *sound bad*, and *taste bad* are considered standard English. Those are verbs of the five senses of seeing, feeling, smelling, hearing, and tasting; and the word *bad* that modifies them in sentences is a predicate adjective, not an adverb.

Predicate adjectives, you recall, follow such linking verbs as *is*, *are*, *was*, and *were*. To refresh your memory, here are examples with the predicate adjectives in italics.

EXAMPLES

- ☐ They were *sorry*.
- ☐ Juanita is *pretty*.
- ☐ Pedro was *hungry*.

Each italicized word in those sentences, each predicate adjective, modifies or describes the subject of the sentence. The same is true of verbs of the senses when the word *bad* is used as the predicate adjective.

EXAMPLES

Correct: ☐ This food smells *bad*.
Correct: ☐ Juanita feels *bad*.

The word *slow* is an adjective; *slowly* is the adverb.

EXAMPLES

Adverb: ☐ He drove *slowly*.
         ☐ He ran *slowly*.
Adjective: ☐ He is a *slow* driver.
            ☐ He ran a *slow* race.

Although *different from* is used more commonly than *different than*, both are considered standard English. Errors do occur when the adjective *different* is used as an adverb.

EXAMPLES

Correct: ☐ Does he do it any differently?
          (The adverb *differently* modifies the verb *do*.)

Incorrect: □   Does he do it any *different*?
(*Different* is an adjective modifying the verb *do*
and thus is incorrect.)

FOR PRACTICE

In the blank by each sentence below, write whether the word in italics in that sentence is an adjective or an adverb.

1. He was *happy* when he came in.   _____
2. He came in *happily*.   _____
3. The explanation is *clear*.   _____
4. He explained the subject *clearly*.   _____
5. He swam *well*.   _____
6. He is a *good* swimmer.   _____
7. The hospital *certainly* needed volunteers. _____
8. He is a *skillful* workman.   _____
9. He works *skillfully*.   _____
10. The company has been in operation
    continuously since 1954.   _____

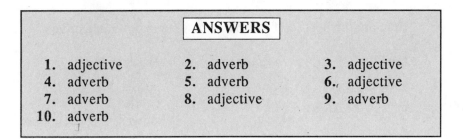

ANSWERS		
1. adjective	2. adverb	3. adjective
4. adverb	5. adverb	6. adjective
7. adverb	8. adjective	9. adverb
10. adverb		

2.16 ADJECTIVES AND ADVERBS HAVE DEGREES OF COMPARISON.

Adjectives and adverbs, with a few exceptions, change form as they are used in comparing two or more items. The three degrees of comparison are *positive*, *comparative*, and *superlative*.

Positive, which indicates no comparison.

EXAMPLE

☐   She is a *pretty* girl.

Comparative, which is comparison between two.

EXAMPLE

☐   She is *prettier* than her sister.

Superlative, which is comparison among more than two.

EXAMPLE

☐   She is the *prettiest* girl in her class.

Here are the degree of comparison of some other adjectives.

Positive	Comparative	Superlative
good, well	better	best
cold	colder	coldest
slow	slower	slowest
active	more active	most active
active	less active	least active

Most adverbs form the comparative and superlative by the use of *more* and *most* or *less* and *least*.

EXAMPLES

rapidly	more rapidly	most rapidly
slowly	more slowly	most slowly
gently	less gently	least gently

■   **The important key to remember is that the comparative is used only when two persons, places, or things are compared; the superlative is used for more than two.**

It would be incorrect to say that Ned is the best player if you are comparing him with William because only two persons are being compared. Correctly, Ned is a better player than William. However, it would be correct to say that Ned is the best if you compare him with more than two or the entire team. Correctly, Ned is the best player on the team.

EXAMPLES

Comparative: □   Leon is a *better* swimmer than Henry.
Superlative: □   Leon is the *best* swimmer on the team.

Comparative: □   Is John or Henry *older*?
Superlative: □   Is John the *oldest* of the three boys?

■   **Adjectives and adverbs that end in *er* for the comparative degree and in *est* for the superlative degree are considered regular.**

An example of a regular adjective follows.

EXAMPLE

□   Jack is a *funny* man. He is *funnier* than David. He is *funniest* of all the comedians here tonight.

An example of a regular adverb is *soon*, with *sooner* as the comparative form and *soonest* as the superlative.

□ Tony will arrive *soon*. He will arrive *sooner* than George.
He may arrive *soonest* of all the workers.

Examples of irregular adjectives are *good* (*better*, *best* — not *gooder*, *goodest*); and *bad* (*worse*, *worst* — not *badder*, *baddest*).

■ **With some adjectives and most adverbs, the comparative is formed by using the *more* or *less* and the superlative by using *most* or *least*.**

EXAMPLE

□ This is a *direct* route to Chicago. It is *more direct* than the route through Louisville. It is the *most direct* of all routes.

■ **The comparative and the superlative of some adjectives may be formed with the endings *er* and *est*, *more* and *most*, or *less* and *least*.**

EXAMPLES

Examples with the word *polite*, and all are correct.

Comparative:	□ Lindsey is *politer* than Fred.
	□ Lindsey is *more polite* than Fred.
	□ Lindsey is *less polite* than Fred.
Superlative:	□ Allen is the *politest* of all the boys.
	□ Allen is the *most polite* of all the boys.
	□ Allen is the *least polite* of all the boys.

■ **When the positive form of an adjective or an adverb contains more than two syllables, the degrees of comparison are always formed by the use of *more* and *most* or *less* and *least*.**

EXAMPLES

□ delicate / more delicate / most delicate
□ comprehensive / less comprehensive / least comprehensive

Some adjectives and adverbs exist only in the positive degree; that is, they cannot be properly used in the comparative or the superlative degree. The word *dead* is an example. One creature cannot be more dead or less dead than another. Also, if something is *impossible*, it cannot be more or less impossible than something else. Or if it is *perfect*, it cannot be more perfect or less perfect than something else. The word *unique* is another example. Such words are considered absolute and thus not comparable. Of course, it is correct to say that a creature is *nearly dead* or that a picture is *almost perfect*; but that is not using degrees of comparison.

Your dictionary lists degrees of comparison for irregular adjectives but not for those that are regular.

EXAMPLES

☐ *poor*, adj. (No other listing is given, so you know that *poor* is regular; that is, poor, poorer, poorest.)

☐ *many*, adj. (This is followed by *more*, *most*, indicating that it is irregular.) Example of its use: many trees, more trees, most trees.

FOR PRACTICE

Underline the correct adjective or adverb in each of these sentences.

1. He is the (taller, tallest) of the two men.
2. I am glad that you came so (quick, quickly) when I called you.
3. Never had the Indians played so (bad, badly) in the past ten years.
4. That was the (funnier, funniest) joke I heard all evening.
5. The team won the game (very easy, very easily).
6. Lillian is able to talk (well, good) since she recovered from her injury.

7. Speak (soft, softly) to that dog.

8. This orange is the (sweeter, sweetest) of the two.

9. James (sure, surely) will come tomorrow.

10. He played the trumpet (real, really) well.

Now check your answers to see how many you have correct.

ANSWERS

1. taller	2. quickly	3. badly	4. funniest
5. very easily	6. well	7. softly	8. sweeter
9. surely	10. really		

2.17   PREPOSITIONS BEGIN PREPOSITIONAL PHRASES.

Prepositions are words everyone uses every day. Here are some of the common ones: *to, at, with, around, between, in, out, into, under, above, among, before, by.*

■ A *preposition*, one of the eight parts of speech, is a word that links or shows relationship of a noun or a pronoun to some other word in the sentence.

The prefix *pre* is from the Latin *prae* which means *before* or *in front of*, so a pre/position is a position before or in front of the word or words that form a prepositional phrase.

■ Prepositions are almost always used in groups of words called *phrases*. A phrase, mentioned in Lesson 1.10, is a group of grammatically related words that has no subject or verb and functions as a part of speech. A phrase that begins with a preposition is called a *prepositional phrase.* It is important that you learn to recognize prepositional phrases.

EXAMPLES

- ☐ *around* the house
- ☐ *under* the table
- ☐ *to* the garden
- ☐ *before* Christmas
- ☐ *down* the steps
- ☐ *near* the tree

FOR PRACTICE

Underline the prepositional phrases in these sentences.

1. We planted flowers around the house but not in the garden.
2. The trees towered above the house.
3. I walked after the dog into the forest.
4. It was a secret between Mary and me.
5. You gave the book to whom?
6. Except for me, all were laughing.
7. I could not attend because of illness.
8. I found the book under the table.
9. The house stood apart from the barn.
10. She gave the book to me.

ANSWERS

1. around the house, in the garden 2. above the house
3. after the dog, into the forest   4. between Mary and me

5. to whom   6. Except for me
7. because of illness   8. under the table
9. from the barn   10. to me

2.18 CONJUNCTIONS SERVE AS CONNECTIVES.

The conjunction is one of the eight parts of speech in English grammar. In Lesson 1.10 you learned that conjunctions are one group of connectives that link words, phrases, clauses, and sentences. Not all words used as connectives are called conjunctions, however.

■ *Coordinating conjunctions* **are used to connect words, phrases, clauses, and sentences of equal grammatical rank.**

EXAMPLES

□ *Cattle* and *sheep* are domesticated animals.

The conjunction *and* in that sentence connects two nouns, *cattle* and *sheep*, to form a compound subject.

□ What I said to him went *in one ear* and *out the other*.
□ *Arriving at the meeting* and *finding no one there*, he returned home.

In each of these sentences two phrases, in italics, are connected by the conjunction *and*.

□ *He tried to unlock the door*, but *he was unable to do so*.

In that sentence the conjunction *but* connects two sentences to from a compound sentence.

■ *Correlative conjunctions* **are always used in pairs.**

EXAMPLES

☐ *Both* Henry *and* James watched the parade.
☐ *Either* we make a profit *or* the project will fail.

In the first sentence two nouns, Henry and James, are connected by the correlative conjunction *both...and* as a compound subject in a simple sentence. In the second, two sentences are connected by the correlative conjunction *either...or* to form a compound sentence.

■ *Conjunctive adverbs* **are also used as connectives in compound sentences.**

EXAMPLE

☐ He tried many times to unlock the door; *finally* he succeeded.

The conjunctive adverb *finally* is used in that sentence to form a compound sentence.

■ *Transitional phrases* **are used as connectives to form compound sentences.**

EXAMPLES

☐ He took all the tools from the box; *what is more*, he kept them.
☐ The two men spent days arguing about the project; *in the meantime*, the case was decided by the court.

Numerous words and phrases are used as transitional expressions. The list in Lesson 1.10 is not all that complete.

As you have learned, there are four kinds of words or groups of words that may be used as connectives to form compound sentences. They are *coordinating conjunctions, correlative conjunctions, conjunctive adverbs*, and *transitional phrases* or *expressions*.

There are only two kinds of connectives for dependent clauses in complex sentences. You learned about them in Lesson 1.10. They are *subordinating conjunctions* and *relative pronouns*.

■ *Subordinating conjunctions* **connect dependent clauses to independent clauses to form complex sentences.**

EXAMPLE

☐ I will go with you *whenever* you are ready.

The subordinating conjunction in that sentence connects the dependent clause to the independent clause to form a complex sentence.

■ *Relative pronouns* **introduce dependent clauses in complex sentences.**

EXAMPLE

☐ It is a store *that* sells exotic plants.

The relative pronoun *that* in that sentence introduces a dependent clause to form a complex sentence.

In standard English it is important to distinguish between conjunctions and prepositions. Common errors are made in the use of *like*, which is a preposition, and *as*, which is a subordinating conjunction.

EXAMPLE

Incorrect: ☐ He acts *like* he owns the place.

In that sentence the preposition *like* is used incorrectly to connect a dependent clause to an independent clause to form a complex sentence. Only a subordinating conjunction or a relative pronoun can properly connect a dependent clause to an independent clause to form a complex sentence.

EXAMPLE

Correct: ☐   He acts *as if* he owns the place.

The subordinating conjunction *as if* is used correctly in that sentence to connect the dependent clause to the independent clause.

The word *like* as a preposition should indicate similarity or resemblance.

EXAMPLES

☐   He works *like* a beaver.
☐   He thinks *like* an adult.

Note that the word *like* in each of those sentences is used as a preposition, as the first word in a prepositional phrase.

FOR PRACTICE

Now see if you can identify the kinds of connectives used in these compound sentences. Fill the blank with A if the connective is a coordinating conjunction, B for correlative conjunction, C for a conjunctive adverb, and D for a transitional phrase. There are two of each.

1. __ I wanted to remain for the second act, but my friends refused to do so.

2. __ We had planned to go to the ball game that day; instead, we stayed at home and worked a crossword puzzle.

3. __ The band came marching by; next, the clowns came into view.

4. __ Whether we deposit the money now or wait until September will make no difference in the interest it earns.

5. __ He offered to take me with him on the cruise; what is more, he said he would pay all my expenses.

6. __ I wanted to go to the game; on the other hand, I had a job that required my remaining at work.

7. __ Not only did he have great wealth, but he was also handsome.

8. __ He wasn't very intelligent, yet he was able to amass a fortune.

Write S in the blank if the dependent clauses in each complex sentence below is connected by a subordinating conjunction and R if it is introduced by a relative pronoun. There are three of each.

9. __ I saw him *before* we left town.

10. __ I will talk with him *after* he arrives.

11. __ This is the book *which* he said he wanted.

12. __ Rice is planted *when* the rainy season begins.

13. __ My brother is the man *who* rescued the dog from drowning.

14. __ This is the telephone number *that* is in the book.

Now check your answers to see how many you have correct.

ANSWERS				
1. A	2. C	3. C	4. B	5. D
6. D	7. B	8. A	9. S	10. S
11. R	12. S	13. R	14. R	

2.19 INTERJECTIONS ARE A WORD OR WORDS "THROWN IN."

■ An *interjection* is a word that expresses feeling or emotion or surprise, but it has no grammatical relationship to other words, phrases, or clauses in the sentence.

EXAMPLES

- □ *Oh*, what a beautiful morning.
- □ *Well*, I will go myself.
- □ *Alas*, the bird is dead.
- □ *Ah*, I see the way now.

The interjections used in those sentences are separated from the remainder of the sentence by commas. It is also correct to use an exclamation point with an interjection.

EXAMPLES

- □ *Ah*! I see the way now.
- □ *Oh*! You don't mean that.

Interjections are often used in speaking but only occasionally in writing. The prefix *inter* means *between* and *jection* is from the Latin *jacere* which means *to throw*, so an interjection is something thrown between or thrown in.

2.20   VERBALS DO NOT FUNCTION AS VERBS.

You have now been introduced to the eight parts of speech, but it would be well at this point to learn about three forms of verbs that are called *verbals*.

■   *Verbals* are verb forms that function not as verbs but as other parts of speech. The names of the three verbals are *infinitives*, *participles*, and *gerunds*.

The following explanation should help you to learn what verbals are and how they are used in sentences.

■ An *infinitive* is simply a verb with the word *to* in front of it. The word *to* used in this manner is called "the sign of the infinitive."

Examples of infinitives are *to go*, *to be*, *to run*, *to jump*, *to swim*.

An infinitive may be used as a noun or as an adverb or as an adjective.

EXAMPLES

☐ *To dance* is fun.
(The infinitive *to dance* is used as a noun — as the subject of the sentence.)

☐ We went to the pool *to swim*.
(The infinitive *to swim* is used as an adverb — it modifies the verb *went* by telling why we went.)

☐ He gave us lessons *to remember*.
(The infinitive *to remember* is used as an adjective; it modifies the noun *lessons* by telling what kind of lessons he gave.)

■ An infinitive may look like a prepositional phrase, but it is quite different. A prepositional phrase always ends with a noun or a pronoun. An infinitive has a verb in it.

In your study of the tense of verbs, you learned that two of the principal parts of a verb are the *present participle* and the *past participle*. You saw that the present participle of a verb always ends with the letters *ing*, and the past participle usually, but not always, ends with the letter *d* or *ed* or *t*.* For example, the present participle of *stop* is *stopping*, and the past participle is *stopped*.

To make this explanation more complete, it should be pointed out that both participles and infinitives have tense. That complicates the

---

* Verbs that end in *d* or *ed* or *t* in the past tense and in the past participle are called *regular verbs*; those with other endings are called *irregular verbs*.

study of grammar even more, but tenses give greater flexibility to the English language. Here are four forms of an infinitive and of a participle.

Tense	Infinitives	Participles
Present tense	to write	writing
Present perfect active	to have written	having written
Present passive	to be written	being written
Present perfect passive	to have been written	having been written

As stated before, a participle in the present tense ends with *ing*. Examples are *going*, *swimming*, *learning*. When such participles are used in the progressive tense in sentences, they need auxiliary or helping verbs, as illustrated in these sentences.

EXAMPLES

  □   He *is going*.
  □   He *has been swimming*.
  □   He *was learning* grammar.

The progressive tense shows continuing action; that is, action in progress. That is easy enough to understand, but verbs ending in *ing* have other uses besides serving as verbs in sentences.

■   **A verb ending in *ing* can serve as an adjective and it can serve as a noun. When it serves as an adjective, it is called a *participle*; and when it serves as a noun, it is called a *gerund*. Participles and gerunds look alike, as they both end in *ing*; but they serve different functions in sentences.**

Here are examples of present participles used as adjectives, with the participles in italics.

EXAMPLES

  □   We like your *swimming* teacher.

- The *running* boy fell to the ground.
- *Standing*, the man seemed very tall.

In those sentences, *swimming* modifies *teacher*, *running* modifies *boy*, and *standing* modifies the noun *man*. The participle (the verbal) in each of those sentences modifies a noun; and as only adjectives can modify nouns, each verbal serves as an adjective.

■ **A past participle, which ends in *d* or *ed*, or *t*, may also be used as an adjective.**

EXAMPLE

- The student, *puzzled* by the question, began to study his text-book.

In that sentence, the word *puzzled* is a past participle used as an adjective to modify the noun *student*.

Here are more examples of past participles used as adjectives, with the past participles in italics.

EXAMPLES

- *Scorned*, he left town.
- *Fatigued*, he went to sleep.
- The player, *confused*, lost the ball.

■ **A participle that serves as a noun is called a *gerund*. In other words, when a participle (a verbal) is used as the subject of a sentence or as a predicate nominative or in any other way as a noun, it is called a gerund.**

EXAMPLES

- *Studying* required concentration.
  (Gerund used as the subject of the sentence.)

☐   His downfall was *gambling*.
(Gerund used as a predicate nominative.)

FOR PRACTICE

Now see if you can sort it out. If the italicized word in the sentence is a gerund (a verbal used as a noun), write Gerund in the blank; if it is a participle (a verbal used as an adjective), write Participle. There are three of each.

1.   The *blooming* rose had faded.   _____

2.   The baby's *crying* annoyed the speaker.   _____

3.   She had *training* wheels on her bicycle.   _____

4.   The *living* trees were beautiful.   _____

5.   *Marching* is part of a soldier's job.   _____

6.   His *going* away made us unhappy.   _____

Underline the infinitives in these sentences.

7.   We wish to buy some candy.

8.   We expected him to have bought the candy by now.

9.   We wish the car to be driven by John.

10.   He wanted to swim in the pool.

11.   If you wish to go, we will leave now.

12.   Whom do you think him to be?

ANSWERS		
1. Participle	2. Gerund	3. Participle
4. Participle	5. Gerund	6. Gerund
7. to buy	8. to have bought	9. to be driven
10. to swim	11. to go	12. to be

REVIEW OF PARTS OF SPEECH

You have now been introduced to the eight parts of speech. This review will help you recall the important points regarding each part of speech.

Despite dictionary labels, words become parts of speech only when they are used in sentences; and it is their use in sentences that determines which parts of speech they are. Many words in the English language may be one part of speech when used in one way and another part of speech when used in another way.

EXAMPLE

☐   The children *play* in the park.

The word *play* can be a verb, as used in this sentence. Or it can be a noun (the name of something) when used in this manner.

☐   We saw the *play* in the theater.

Sentence Essentials

Essential for a complete sentence (a complete thought) are a subject, which may be a noun or a pronoun or a group of words used as a noun, and a verb.

1. *Noun* means name.

■   **A noun may be proper, which means it names a specific person or thing; it may be common, which means it names one of a group of persons or things.   A proper noun begins with a capital letter; a common noun begins with a small letter.**

EXAMPLES

☐   The *glass* is empty.   (common noun)
☐   I love *Cheryl.*   (proper noun)

■ **Nouns have number. They are either singular or plural.**

EXAMPLES

☐ That *tree* is an oak.   (singular number)
☐ The *trees* are green.   (plural number)

2. **A *pronoun* stands for a noun or another pronoun.**

EXAMPLES

☐ *Jennifer* is my friend; I like *her*.
   The word *her* is the pronoun; it stands for *Jennifer*.

■ **Personal pronouns have *person, number, gender,* and *case*.**

EXAMPLES

☐ Brenda is my friend; *I* like *her*.
   In that sentence the pronoun *I* is first person, the pronoun *her* is third person.

☐ *I* asked *them* to go with *me*.
   In that sentence the pronouns *I* and *me* are singular; the pronoun *them* is plural.

☐ *He* is older than *she*.
   In that sentence the pronoun *He* is masculine; the pronoun *she* is feminine.

Case is explained in Chapter 3.

3. ***Verbs* are of two kinds. One kind of verb shows action; the other kind shows a relationship or condition.**

EXAMPLES

- ☐ She *stirred* the coffee.
  (verb shows action)
- ☐ The coffee *was* strong.
  (verb shows a condition, not an action)

4. An *adjective* is a word that describes or modifies a noun or a pronoun.

EXAMPLES

- ☐ the *purple* flower
- ☐ the *fast* car
- ☐ a *tall* man

5. An *adverb* is a word that describes or modifies a verb, an adjective, or another adverb.

EXAMPLES

- ☐ She speaks *softly*.
  (The adverb *softly* modifies the verb *speaks* by telling how she speaks.)
- ☐ Joe was *very* poor.
  (The adverb *very* modifies the adjective *poor*, and *poor* modifies the noun *Joe*.)
- ☐ She speaks *very* softly.
  (The adverb *very* modifies the adverb *softly* which modifies the verb *speaks*.)

Connectives

6. A *preposition* is a word that shows the relation of a noun or a pronoun to another word in the sentence.

That is the definition; but more important than being able to define prepositions is being able to recognize them, especially as they are used in phrases. A preposition introduces a prepositional phrase; it almost always comes first.

EXAMPLES

Preposition	Prepositional Phrase
with	He came *with us.*
by	She sat *by them.*
in	I saw the bird *in the tree.*
around	He drove *around the block.*

7. A *conjunction* is a word that links or connects words, sentences, and parts of sentences.

EXAMPLES

- ☐ Melissa *and* Sarah went to school.
  (The conjunction *and* connects two proper nouns to form a compound subject.)

- ☐ Carrie sang *and* played.
  (The conjunction *and* connects two verbs to form a compound predicate.)

- ☐ I went to school, *but* Thomas remained at home.
  (The conjunction *but* connects two independent clauses to form a compound sentence.)

Interrupters

8. An *interjection* is a word or words "thrown in." It stands alone, with no grammatical relation to the remainder of the sentence.

EXAMPLES

- ☐ Bravo!
- ☐ Alas!
- ☐ Gee!
- ☐ Oh!
- ☐ Oh, I cut my finger.

FOR PRACTICE

Underline the parts of speech in these sentences.

1. *Noun.* The bird flew away.

2. *Pronoun.* Jane saw it fly away.

3. *Verb.* It flew to a tree.

4. *Adverb.* The bird sings sweetly.

5. *Adjective.* The bird is blue.

6. *Preposition.* It lives near the garden.

7. *Conjunction.* I saw him but he did not see me.

8. *Adverb.* He spoke softly.

9. *Interjection.* Bravo! You are the winner.

10. *Verb.* He has gone away.

ANSWERS			
1. bird	2. it	3. flew	4. sweetly
5. blue	6. near	7. but	8. softly
9. Bravo!	10. has gone		

MORE REVIEW

You have learned that verbals are verb forms used not as verbs but as other parts of speech. The three verbals are participles, gerunds, and infinitives.

■ **A *participle* is a verb that ends in *ing* and is used as an adjective.**

EXAMPLE

□ The *flashing* lights blinded me.
(The participle *flashing* modifies the subject noun *lights*, so it is used as an adjective.)

■ **A *gerund* is a verb that ends in *ing* and is used as a noun.**

EXAMPLE

□ *Dancing* is great fun.
(The gerund *dancing* is used as a noun, the subject of the sentence.)

■ **An *infinitive* is a verb with the word *to* in front of it. It is used as a noun, as an adverb, and sometimes as an adjective.**

EXAMPLES

□ *To err* is human; *to forgive* is divine.
(In that compound sentence, the infinitives *to err* and *to forgive* are the subjects and thus used as nouns.)

□ He went to the store *to buy* groceries.
(In that sentence the infinitive *to buy* is used as an adverb. It modifies the verb *went* by telling why he went.)

☐   He gave me permission *to enter.*
(In that sentence the infinitive *to enter* is used as an adjective to modify the noun *permission.*)

TEST ON PARTS OF SPEECH

After the review take this test to see how much of the material you have mastered.

Underline the simple subject (one word) in each sentence.

1. Who will do the work?
2. Skipping the rope is good exercise.
3. I saw Nadia in the garden.
4. Most of the trees were green.
5. While still a boy, my uncle joined the Navy.

Underline the verbs in these sentences. Some are more than one word.

6. Barbara knelt in the chapel.
7. She was kneeling when we arrived.
8. We could not leave before noon.
9. I should have been there.
10. He wanted to buy a red car.

Underline the compound subjects in these sentences.

11. Swimming and hiking are enjoyable exercises.
12. Hard work and honesty lead toward success.
13. My friend and her daughter were visiting us.
14. If you go, Mary and Sue should go with you.
15. Reading, writing, and arithmetic are taught in school.

Underline the compound predicates (verbs only) in these simple sentences.

16. She gave me a present and then helped me unwrap it.
17. I had two dollars but needed three to buy the ticket.
18. The price increases and decreases with a change in supply.
19. They rode part way and walked the rest of the way.
20. The student walked into the room and took his seat.

Draw a slanting line between the complete subject and the predicate in each of these sentences.

21. The man in the moon came down too soon.
22. Sewing is easy for me.
23. *Going My Way* is the title of a motion picture.
24. Captain Anderson, a tall man, met us at the station.
25. The rain fell in torrents.

Underline the subordinate clauses in these sentences.

26. When I was young, I lived in Boston.
27. Bernard, who is my brother, arrived home late.
28. If you want to succeed, you will have to work hard.
29. The cattle were grazing where the grass was green.
30. That little girl, whom we all love, is six years old.

Underline the main clauses in these complex sentences.

31. I work because I need the money.
32. When he was eight years old, he won a prize in spelling.
33. If you wish to attend, you are free to do so.
34. I washed the dishes after he had gone home.
35. The author who wrote the book visited the library yesterday.

Punctuate these sentences as needed with commas and semicolons.

36. I found the book on the shelf where I had placed it weeks ago.

37. It is a beautiful book however I could not read it because it is written in Greek.

38. I gave it to my friend he can read Greek.

39. While he was in the garden looking at the flowers I was in the study reading my lesson in history.

40. The general agreed to come alone instead he brought two bodyguards.

Underline each word that should be capitalized in these sentences.

41. the title of the book is *the power of positive thinking*.

42. he is a member of the lions club.

43. dale joined the u. s. navy in april.

44. we saw the tower of london in the distance.

45. labor day is always on a monday.

Write the plurals of these nouns.

46. goose   _____

47. hospital   _____

48. leaf   _____

49. genius   _____

50. tax   _____

51. governor general   _____

52. Japanese   _____

53. giraffe   _____

54. businessman   _____

55. criterion   _____

Underline the pronouns in these sentences.

56. I gave her my watch.

57. His father works while he plays.

58. The woman who does the cleaning is coming tomorrow.

59. The man whom we talked to in the store in my neighbor.

60. We met the lady and we liked her.

Underline the antecedents of the pronouns italicized in these sentences.

61. The man *whom* we talked to in the store in my neighbor.

62. The car *that* was stolen is a Corvette.

63. The man asked me to give *him* some money.

64. Carolyn and Marie ate *their* supper at home.

65. Martha, *who* lives in the city, arrived late.

Underline the adjectives in these sentences.

66. He had two books with him.

67. One book had a red cover.

68. Both men had new cars.

69. It was a Hungarian dance.

70. There was a sudden change in the weather.

Place hyphens as needed in the compound adjectives in these sentences.

71. The police made a house to house search for the three year old girl.

72. The child was wearing a blue green dress.

73. The actress had a peaches and cream complexion and a well trained singing voice.

74. After her tour she took a much needed rest in a so called spa.

75. The old man was carrying a five foot fishing rod and a well thumbed Spanish dictionary.

Underline the adverbs in these sentences.

76. He walked slowly along the road.

77. The weather changed suddenly.

78. Darrell is an unusually fast reader.

79. If you walk rapidly, you can arrive before the train leaves.

80. He is perfectly happy.

Underline the prepositional phrases in these sentences.

81. There was a sudden change in the weather.

82. He had two books with him.

83. Linda walked around the car.

84. She went to the theater to see a play.

85. The letters are difficult to read in the dark.

Underline the infinitives in these sentences.

86. I want to go home.

87. He turned the corner quickly to avoid an accident.

88. Do you want to read your story now?

89. I'll show you how to repair your typewriter.

90. He watched with interest as the bird tried to build a nest on the swaying branches.

If the italicized word is a participle, write P in the blank; if it is a gerund, write G in the blank.

91. He approves of your *reading* the poem.   _____

92. *Standing* on the hill, he could see a great distance.   _____

93. *Drifting* with the current is pleasant.   _____

94. *Flying* made him nervous.   _____

95. He said he did not trust a *flying* machine.   _____

If the italicized word is transitive, write T in the blank; if it is intransitive, write I in the blank.

96. Whom *will* you *see* at the bank?   _____

97. The man in the car *is* my brother.   _____

98. This milk *tastes* sour.   _____

99. He *walked* for an hour.   _____

100. Jose *hit* a home run with all the bases full.   _____

Underline the correct form of the verb in parentheses in these sentences.

101. (Lie, Lay) the book on the table.

102. Come (sit, set) by me.

103. The hen was (sitting, setting) on the nest.

104. He was (lying, laying) in bed.

105. (Sit, Set) the dish on the table.

Check your answers.

ANSWERS		
1. Who	2. Skipping	3. I
4. Most	5. uncle	6. knelt
7. was kneeling		8. could leave
9. should have been		10. wanted
11. Swimming, hiking		12. work, honesty
13. friend, daughter		14. Mary, Sue
15. Reading, writing, arithmetic		16. gave, helped

17. had, needed
18. increases, decreases
19. rode, walked
20. walked, took
21. The man in the moon / came down too soon.
22. Sewing / is easy for me.
23. *Going My Way* / is the title of a motion picture.
24. Captain Anderson, a tall man, / met us at the station.
25. The rain / fell in torrents.
26. When I was young
27. who is my brother
28. If you want to succeed
29. where the grass was green
30. whom we all love
31. I work
32. he won a prize in spelling
33. you are free to do so.
34. I washed the dishes
35. The author visited the library yesterday.
36. No internal punctuation needed
37. book; however,
38. friend;
39. flowers,
40. alone; instead,
41. The title of the book is *The Power of Positive Thinking.*
42. He is a member of the Lions Club.
43. Dale joined the U. S. Navy in April.
44. We saw the Tower of London in the distance.
45. Labor Day is always on a Monday.
46. geese
47. hospitals
48. leaves
49. geniuses or genii
50. taxes
51. governors general
52. Japanese
53. giraffes
54. businessmen
55. criteria
56. I, her, my
57. His, he
58. who
59. whom, we, my
60. We, we, her
61. man
62. car
63. man
64. Carolyn and Marie
65. Martha
66. two
67. One, red
68. Both, new
69. Hungarian
70. sudden
71. house-to-house, three-year-old
72. blue-green
73. peaches-and-cream, well-trained
74. much-needed, so-called
75. five-foot, well-thumbed

76. slowly	**77.** suddenly
78. unusually	**79.** rapidly
80. perfectly	**81.** in the weather
82. with him	**83.** around the car.
84. to the theater	**85.** in the dark

86. to go   **87.** to avoid   **88.** to read
89. to repair   **90.** to build
91. G   **92.** P   **93.** G   **94.** G   **95.** P
96. T   **97.** I   **98.** I   **99.** I   **100.** T
101. Lay   **102.** sit   **103.** sitting
104. lying   **105.** Set

3

CASE

Up to this point you have been learning the basics, the fundamentals of grammar. In following lessons you can begin to apply what you have learned, starting with the study of *case*. Case refers to the form of a noun or pronoun that shows its relationship to other words in the sentence. Note that only nouns and pronouns have case. The three cases are nominative, objective, and possessive. The first lesson explains nominative case.

3.1 THE SUBJECT OF A VERB IS ALWAYS IN THE NOMINATIVE CASE.

■ **Nouns and pronouns have *case*. That means that they change form depending on the way they are used in sentences. The three cases are *nominative*, *objective*, and *possessive*.**

Nouns do not change for nominative and objective cases, but they do change for possessive case. Most personal pronouns, however, change for all three cases; and that is why many mistakes are made in their use.

The way personal pronouns and the pronoun *who* change form for case is shown in the box in Lesson 2.3. There you saw these pronouns:

Nominative Case	Objective Case	Possessive Case
I	me	my, mine
you	you	your, yours
he, she, it	him, her, it	his, her, hers, its
we	us	our, ours
they	them	their, theirs
who	whom	whose

There are four rules for use of the nominative case. One of the rules is explained in this lesson, the others in the next lesson.

■ **Rule 1. The subject of a verb is always in the nominative case.**

You have learned that a sentence always has a subject, which is what the sentence (the complete thought) is about; and it always has a verb.

EXAMPLES

The subject of a verb may be a noun.

- □ *Andrew* tore the page.
- □ *The cat* caught a mouse.

The subject may be groups of words (a phrase).

- □ *Visiting my aunt in Boston* was always enjoyable.

The subject may be a pronoun.

- □ *He* kicked the ball.
- □ *She* was enjoyable to visit.

Subjects that are of most concern are pronouns, because as stated before, personal pronouns and the pronoun *who* change for case. Most mistakes are made in using objective case when the nominative case should be used and in using the nominative case when the objective case should be used.

EXAMPLE

- □ Carrie and I were in a hurry.

The verb in that sentence is *were*. The subject of the verb is *Carrie and I*. The pronoun *I* is nominative, which is correct because it is part of the subject of the verb. It would be incorrect to say *Carrie and me* because *me* is always in the objective case.

The rule states that the subject of the verb is always in the nominative case, and that every verb has a subject. The subject is not always easy to locate, however, because it may be separated in a sentence from the verb.

EXAMPLES

- □ Persons who *are* agile *can play* handball quite well.

That sentence has two verbs. The first is *are* and the subject is *who*, which is in the nominative case. The second verb is *can play* and its subject is *Persons*. Sometimes it helps to determine the subjects of verbs by breaking the sentences up in this manner:

> Persons *can play* handball
> who *are* agile

☐ The man who they *believed was* the cause of the fire *is* now in prison.

That sentence has three verbs, and each verb has a subject. The subject of the verb *believed* is *they*. The subject of the verb *was* is *who*. The subject of the verb *is* is *The man*. Read it this way:

> The man *is* now in prison
> who *was* the cause of the fire
> they *believed*

☐ The children who he *said were swimming* that day *were* really *playing* in the yard.

The sentence has three verbs: *said, were swimming, were playing.*

Now you can break it into subjects and verbs:

> The children *were* really *playing* in the yard
> who *were swimming* that day
> he *said*

The subjects are, respectively, *children, who, he.*

FOR PRACTICE

Find the simple subject of each italicized verb in these sentences.

EXAMPLE

☐   The reason I *liked* him *is* that he *was* polite.

Answer: reason *is*, I *liked*, he *was*

1. Leo and he *went* to Chicago where they *expected* to meet us.
2. Although they *were* mistaken, they *continued* to argue.
3. If they *are* successful, they *will set* a new record.
4. The man whom we *saw was wearing* a green shirt.
5. She *is* the kind of nurse who they *thought would take* good care of their mother.

Next underline the correct pronoun in each of these sentences, keeping in mind that the subjects of verbs are always nominative. Refer to the list on page 154 as needed.

6. (Us, We) girls were in the swimming pool.
7. I was surprised when Henry and (she, her) told us where they had been.
8. Joe and (I, me) didn't think he was telling the truth.
9. During the game, the women and (we, us) men shouted and cheered.
10. The speaker (who, whom) people thought was Irish was actually a German.
11. Were you and (he, him) planning to attend the concert?
12. Yesterday I saw two women (who, whom) I think are sisters.

ANSWERS

1. Leo and he *went*, they *expected*
2. they *were*, they *continued*
3. they *are*, they *will set*
4. we *saw*, man *was wearing*

5. She *is*, they *thought*, who *would take*
6. *We* were
7. *she* told
8. *I* didn't think
9. *we* shouted
10. *who* was Irish
11. you and *he* were planning
12. *who* are sisters

3.2 THE NOMINATIVE CASE IS USED AFTER FORMS OF THE VERB *BE*.

In the previous lesson you were told that there are four rules for the use of the nominative case, but only one rule was explained. It states that the subject of a verb is always in the nominative case.

■ **Rule 2. Use the nominative case for the complement of the verb *be*.**

The verb *be* has many forms: *am, is, are, was, were, shall be, will be, have been, has been, had been, shall have been, will have been.* Those verbs show no action; they only link the predicate to the subject. Some grammarians call them *verbs of being*.

In Lesson 2.9 you learned that there are two kinds of predicate complements for linking verbs, predicate adjectives and predicate nominatives.

EXAMPLE

☐ He is *strong*.

The word *strong* in that sentence is an adjective that describes (modifies) the subject *He*. Used in this manner, it is called a *predicate adjective*. As adjectives do not have case and therefore do not change form when used as predicate complements, they cause little difficulty.

EXAMPLE

□   He is *a soldier*.

The complement in that sentence is *a soldier*; and as *soldier* is a noun, the complement is called a *predicate nominative*. The noun is in the nominative case, but that poses no problem because nouns don't change except for possessive case.

Pronouns, however, do change for case; and as stated before, that is where mistakes are often made.

EXAMPLE

□   It was *she* who cooked the meal.

In that sentence the word *she* is the predicate complement (the predicate nominative) and is in the nominative case. As stated before, forms of the verb *be* are always followed by the nominative form of the pronoun.

EXAMPLES

□   The guests were Mary and I. (not Mary and me)
(The linking verb is *were*; the predicate complements, in the nominative case, are *Mary and I*, the predicate nominatives.)

□   We were surprised when we learned that the mystery guest was *he*. (not him)
(The linking verb is *was*; the predicate complement, in the nominative case, is *he*, the predicate nominative.)

Now you come to the last two rules regarding the case of nouns and pronouns.

■   **Rule 3.   Use the nominative case when the pronoun (or noun) is the object of the infinitive *to be* and the infinitive has no subject.**

□   I was thought to be *he*. (not *him*)
□   He was thought to be *I*. (not *me*)

This is a special case and is explained more fully in Lesson 3.6.

■   **Rule 4. A noun or pronoun in apposition is in the same case as the noun or pronoun it explains or identifies.**

□   Maria, *an attractive girl*, was our waitress.

□   My brother's farm, *a hundred acres of grassland*, is in Iowa.

□   That girl, *she on the flying trapeze*, has been a circus performer since childhood.

The italicized portions of those sentences are called **appositives**. They modify or describe the nouns they modify and are in the same case as the nouns they modify. In the first sentence, the subject *Maria* is in the nominative case and so is the noun *girl*, which is in apposition. In the second sentence the noun *farm* is in the nominative case as the subject of the sentence and so is *grassland*, which is in apposition. In the third sentence *girl* is in the nominative case as the subject of the sentence and so is the pronoun *she*, which is in apposition.

Appositives are explained more fully in Lesson 4.4.

FOR PRACTICE

Underline the correct predicate nominative in each of these sentences.

1. It was (they, them) who rang the doorbell.

2. He is sure the winners will be (we, us).

3. The mystery guest was (he, him).

4. The only volunteers have been Louise and (I, me).

5. (Who, Whom) do you think he is?

To test yourself further, write a letter P in the blank if the italicized pronoun is a predicate nominative and the S if it is the subject of a verb. There are five of each.

6. __ Who is *he*?

7. __ I don't care *who* he is.

8. __ Were you and *he* planning to go swimming?

9. __ The nurse *who* is coming to help is my cousin.

10. __ I am *he* who called.

11. __ Was it *they* who called?

12. __ He is the mechanic *who* will repair our car.

13. __ You should know that *she* will be happy as a nurse.

14. __ It was *I* who locked the door.

15. __ *Who* did you say is going?

ANSWERS				
1. they	2. we	3. he	4. I	5. who
6. P	7. P	8. S	9. S	10. P
11. P	12. S	13. S	14. P	15. S

3.3 FIVE RULES GOVERN THE USE OF THE OBJECTIVE CASE.

A noun or a pronoun is in the objective case when it is:
1. the object of a verb
2. the object of a preposition
3. the indirect object of a verb
4. the subject or object of an infinitive
5. the object of a gerund.

■ **Rule 1. The direct object of a verb is in the objective case.**

You have learned that there are transitive and intransitive verbs, and that transitive verbs have objects and intransitive verbs do not have objects. The object of a transitive verb is the person, place, or thing that receives the action of the verb.

EXAMPLES

- □   Alex saw the ball.
- □   He threw the ball.
- □   She caught the ball.
- □   They kicked the ball.

The object of the transitive verb in each of those sentences is *ball*. The ball received the action of the transitive verb, and so it is called the direct object of the verb.

You recall in your study of verbs in Lesson 2.10 learning that some verbs do not have objects. They show action, but they do not exert any action on an object.

EXAMPLE

- □   The stars *twinkle* in the heavens.

A person, place, or thing can't be *twinkled*, so the verb cannot have an object; that is, it can't have a receiver of the action of twinkling.

The same is true of *smiled* or *laughed*. You can smile sweetly or laugh loudly, but you can't smile something or laugh something.

Verbs of that kind are called *intransitive*, but there are some action verbs that may either be transitive or intransitive, that may or may not have objects, depending on how they are used in sentences.

EXAMPLES

☐   The pelican flies gracefully.
    (The verb *flies* has no object, so the verb is intransitive in this sentence.)

☐   The pilot flies the plane.
    (The *plane* is the object of the verb *flies*; it receives the action of the verb, so the verb is transitive here.)

☐   He runs rapidly.
    (The verb *runs* has no object and is intransitive.)

☐   He runs the company.
    (*The company* is the object of the verb *runs*, so the verb *runs* is transitive.)

The rule is that the object of a verb, the receiver of the action of the verb, is in the objective case. As nouns have the same form in both the nominative and objective cases, this is not a problem; but pronouns can be a problem because they change form.

EXAMPLES

☐   I like *her*.
☐   The teacher told *Nicole* and *me* to go home.
☐   *Whom* did he ask?

Each italicized word in those sentences is the object of the verb. In the second sentence, there are two objects of the verb. In the third sentence, which asks a question, it is easier to determine the subject and the object of the verb by changing the question to a statement, to read this way: He did ask *whom*? When it is stated that way, you can see that *whom* is the object of the verb *ask*.

Nominative and Objective Cases of Pronouns	
Nominative	*Objective*
I	me
who	whom
they	them
she	her
we	us
he	him

FOR PRACTICE

Circle the object of the verb in italics in each of these sentences.

1. Mother, whom *did* you *invite*?
2. He *gave* a present to her.
3. Whom *shall* we *elect* as president?
4. His conduct *pleases* both Mary and me.
5. Isn't it pleasant to have a helper whom you *can trust*?
6. The man whom we *saw* in the park is a doctor.
7. The bank *sent* me a check last week.

Underline the correct object of the verb in each of these sentences. Refer to the chart above when necessary.

8. She sent my sister and (I, me) to the park to play.
9. (Who, Whom) did you invite to the party?
10. She asked the three brothers and (we, us) to go home.
11. Who told you and (they, them) about the accident?
12. We cautioned the boy and (she, her) about talking too much.

13. The guard rushed Henry and (I, me) through the gate.

14. She told (who, whom) about the money?

15. The man said that the woman (who, whom) he had helped had disappeared.

16. The guide led Tom and (I, me) to the exhibit.

17. You saw (who, whom) in the park?

If you are still having difficulty in deciding whether a noun or a pronoun is the subject or the object of a verb, use the method shown in Lesson 3.1 which shows how to break up the sentence to make the subject and the object of the verb clearer. Sentence 15 above will illustrate.

EXAMPLE

The man said
the woman had disappeared
he had helped whom

In this way you can see that *whom* is the object of the verb *had helped*. A simpler sentence is number 9 above, which might read as follows:

☐   You did invite whom to the party.

That shows clearly that *whom* is the object of the verb *did invite*.

ANSWERS

1. whom (object of *did invite*; you did invite whom)
2. a present (object of *gave*)
3. Whom (object of *shall elect*)
4. Mary and me (object of *pleases*)
5. whom (object of *can trust*; you can trust whom)

6. whom (object of *saw*; we saw whom)
7. a check (object of sent; *sent* a check)

8. me	9. Whom	10. us	11. them
12. her	13. me	14. whom	15. whom
16. me	17. whom		

3.4 OBJECTS OF PREPOSITIONS ARE EASY TO FIND.

■   **Rule 2. A noun or pronoun that is the object of a preposition is in the objective case.**

This is simple because it is easy to determine the objects of prepositions. When you studied Parts of Speech, you learned that a prepositional phrase is a group of two or more words that begins with a preposition.

EXAMPLES

☐   He gave the pen *to me*.
☐   I threw it *toward him*.
☐   *About whom* are you talking?
☐   We walked *around them*.

In each of those sentences, the object of the preposition is a pronoun, and each pronoun is in the objective case. The object of a preposition, however, may be any of the following:

A noun	☐	They spoke *to Pedro*.
An adjective	☐	Betty kept the burner *on low*.
An infinitive	☐	She wanted to do nothing *except to eat*.
A participle	☐	You help most *by encouraging him*.
A prepositional phrase	☐	We saw him come *from around the bend*.
A dependent clause	☐	The prize goes *to whoever arrives first*.

FOR PRACTICE

Underline the objects of prepositions in these sentences.

1. It was a secret between Cheryl and me.
2. I gave the money to him.
3. The prize was awarded to Sharon.
4. There was no one there besides them.
5. He asked to whom I gave the book.

Underline the correct pronoun in each of these sentences.

6. For (who, whom) did you vote?
7. It was to (they, them) that we sent the message.
8. After we left, they followed after (we, us).
9. I wanted to give the prize to Helen and (he, him).
10. Lindsey went with Andrew and (I, me) to the show.
11. All of (we, us) miners were on strike.
12. They came especially to visit her and (I, me).
13. With (who, whom) have you talked about the project?
14. I want him to go with Mary and you and (I, me).
15. The money will be divided between you and (I, me).

ANSWERS			
1. Cheryl and me		2. him	3. Sharon
4. them	5. whom	6. whom	7. them
8. us	9. him	10. me	11. us
12. me	13. whom	14. me	15. me

3.5 THE INDIRECT OBJECT RECEIVES THE ACTION INDIRECTLY.

■ **Rule 3. The indirect object of a verb is in the objective case.**

The direct object of the verb tells who or what received the action of the verb. The indirect object tells to whom or for whom the verb's action was done.

EXAMPLE

☐ David sent *me* a check.

The word *me* is the indirect object of the verb *sent*; *a check* is direct object of the verb. David didn't send *me*; he sent *the check*. Generally, the indirect object could just as easily be written as a prepositional phrase, in this way: David sent the check *to me*. Whether it is the indirect object of the verb or the object of a preposition, the noun or pronoun is always in the objective case.

EXAMPLES

Indirect Object	*Prepositional Phrase*
☐ I baked her a cake.	☐ I baked a cake for her.
☐ I bought Helen a gift.	☐ I bought a gift for Helen.
☐ I gave him a gift.	☐ I gave a gift to him.

FOR PRACTICE

Underline the indirect objects in these sentences.

1. He handed me his coat.
2. I will send them a letter.

3. He brought me the car.

4. I will buy Brenda a new dress.

5. You offered whom a choice?

6. My father taught me English.

7. She asked me a question.

8. Irene wrote Robert a letter.

9. Please pass me the cake.

10. He refused Jane the request.

Now check your answers.

ANSWERS

1. me	**2.** them	**3.** me	**4.** Brenda
5. whom	**6.** me	**7.** me	**8.** Robert
9. me	**10.** Jane		

3.6 INFINITIVES MAY HAVE SUBJECTS AND OBJECTS.

■ **Rule 4. The subject and the object of an infinitive are in the objective case, with one small exception.**

You learned that an infinitive is a verb with the word *to* in front of it. Examples are *to go, to swim, to play, to think*. Those examples are formed with the present tense (base form) of the verb; but you learned in Lesson 2.20 that infinitives may have other forms, such as t*o have written*, t*o be written*, and *to have been written*.

You also have learned that a verb in a sentence always has a subject and that it may have an object. An infinitive may have a subject and it may have an object, but unlike a verb it does not necessarily have a subject or an object.

- ☐ I would like to leave.
- ☐ He ordered us to leave.
- ☐ I ordered him to leave us.

The infinitive in each of those sentences is *to leave*. In the first sentence the infinitive has no subject and no object. In the second sentence, *us* is the subject of the infinitive. In the third sentence, *him* is the subject and *us* is the object of the infinitive.

- ☐ He wanted me *to give* him the book.

The subject of the infinitive *to give* in that sentence is *me*. At first it may appear that *me* is the object of the verb *wanted*, but he did not want me; rather, he wanted the book.

Now about the "tiny exception." It occurs with the infinitive *to be*. You have learned that the verb *be* is rather special. You recall that its present tense forms are *am*, *is*, *are*; the past tense forms are *was*, *were*; and the future, *will be*. Such forms of *to be* show relationships, not action.

You learned in Lesson 3.2 that those verbs are always followed by the nominative form of the pronoun.

- ☐ The guests were Wanda and *I*. (not *me*)
- ☐ We were surprised when we learned that the mystery guest was *he*. (not *him*)

In contrast, the subject and the object of the infinitive *to be* are always in the objective case, except when that infinitive has no subject. Then the object is in the nominative case. That is the tiny exception.

■ **Rule. The object of the infinitive *to be* is in the nominative case when the infinitive has no subject. These sentences will illustrate.**

EXAMPLES

☐ He wanted *whom* to be the leader?
☐ I am supposed to be *who*? or
☐ *Who* am I supposed to be?

In the first sentence the subject of the infinitive *to be* is *whom*, which is the objective form of the pronoun, and the object of the infinitive is *the leader*. In the second sentence the infinitive *to be* has no subject, so the object, *who*, is nominative.

Nouns and pronouns are most commonly the subjects and the objects of infinitives. That is not always true, however, because infinitives are used in a number of grammatical constructions.

The subject of an infinitive may be any of the following:

A noun	☐ We want *Lisa* to come with us.
A pronoun	☐ We want *her* to come with us.
A gerund	☐ We think *walking* to be good exercise.
An infinitive	☐ He says *to walk* to be outdoors.
A dependent clause	☐ He said *that I wished to remain silent* to be evidence of my guilt.

The object of an infinitive may be any of the following.

A noun	☐ We wanted to tell *Sarina*.
A pronoun	☐ We wanted to help *her*.
A gerund	☐ We urged her to go *swimming*.
A dependent clause	☐ We wanted to go *where she is*.

Most important is being able to recognize the pronouns that are subjects and objects of infinitives and, with a single exception, take the objective case. Only pronouns change form for the objective case. Nouns change only for possessive case.

FOR PRACTICE

Underline the infinitives in these sentences.

1. I wanted to go with him.
2. I wanted him to buy me a hat.
3. He told me to drive the car.
4. Whom do you wish to see?
5. I wanted him to know that we would be there.

Underline the subjects of these infinitives.

6. It is an interesting movie *to watch*.
7. I wanted him *to teach* me.
8. They told Gloria and me *to go* home.
9. Whom did they tell *to go* home?
10. He asked John *to be* quiet.

Underline the objects of these infinitives.

11. He said I would have *to give* the book to Isabel.
12. Whom was he supposed *to ask* for the money?
13. Whom do you think him *to be*?
14. They were believed *to be* we.
15. Whom did you believe her *to be*?

Note that the infinitive *to be* in number 14 has no subject, so the object is in the nominative case. In number 15, the infinitive *to be* has a subject (*her*), so its object is in the objective case.

```
                          ┌─────────────┐
                          │   ANSWERS   │
                          └─────────────┘

   1.  to go           2.  to buy            3.  to drive
   4.  to see          5.  to know           6.  movie
   7.  him             8.  Gloria and me     9.  Whom
  10.  John           11.  the book         12.  Whom
  13.  Whom           14.  we               15.  Whom
```

3.7   A GERUND MAY HAVE AN OBJECT.

■ **Rule 5. The object of a gerund is in the objective case.**

A gerund, you recall, is a verb that ends in *ing* and is used as a noun; that is, it is used as the name of something. A participle is also a verb that ends in *ing* but differs from a gerund in that it describes a person, place, or thing; that is, it is used as an adjective.

EXAMPLES

Gerunds

☐ I like her *singing*.
☐ Ronny worried about *losing* his money.

Participles

☐ The *singing* bird flew away.
☐ It is hard to be on a *losing* team.

Although a gerund is used as a noun and as such may be the subject of a verb or the object of a verb, it also may have an object itself.

EXAMPLES

Subject of a verb: ☐ *Hiking* is fun.
Object of a verb: ☐ Louise loves *hiking*.
Gerund with an object: ☐ *Finding* her at home again was a great pleasure.

All three are simple sentences. The gerunds *hiking* and *finding* are names of actions and thus are considered nouns.

The verb in the third sentence is *was* and the subject is the gerund phrase, *Finding her home again*. The gerund is *Finding*, and the object of the gerund is *her*.

You have learned that the objective case is used for:

1. the object of a transitive verb
2. the indirect object of a verb
3. the object of a preposition
4. the subject of an infinitive
5. the object of an infinitive, and now
6. as the object of a gerund.

The first five are important because it is in those constructions that errors frequently occur. The last one, however, is of lesser importance because no one with a knowledge of the English language is likely to use any case except objective after a gerund.

The various grammatical uses of the gerund can be illustrated with the word *swimming*, which is the name of an activity and hence a noun. As a verbal, it is a gerund. Here are examples of its various uses in sentences.

EXAMPLES

The subject of a sentence: □ *Swimming* is fun.

The object of a verb: □ She likes *swimming*.

A predicate nominative: □ The exercise was *swimming*.

Object of a preposition: □ She often talks *about swimming*.

Object of an infinitive: □ She likes to be *swimming*.

Although a gerund is one word, gerunds are also used to introduce gerund phrases.

EXAMPLES

☐ *Teaching school* is a rewarding occupation.
(subject of the sentence)
☐ He was amused by *hearing the joke.*
(object of the preposition)

Gerunds do not change form so they present no problem. It is well, however, to know that a noun or pronoun before a gerund should usually be in the possessive case.

EXAMPLES

☐ *His* telling about the adventure was interesting.
☐ We were pleased with *Janet's* learning to play the piano.

This is explained further in Lesson 3.9.

FOR PRACTICE

The gerunds in these sentences are in italics. So that you may be able to identify them better, circle the objects of the gerunds.

1. *Teaching* him was not my problem.
2. *Seeing* them rejoice made me happy.
3. *Finding* him alone was fortunate.
4. By *using* drawings, he explained the problem clearly.
5. In *training* dogs, a person needs patience.
6. *Floating* the logs across the lake was difficult.
7. We took turns *persuading* him to sign the agreement.
8. *Presenting* the evidence convinced him that I was right.
9. *Bringing* the tools helped greatly in completing the work.
10. *Moving* the date posed a problem.

ANSWERS

1. him 2. them 3. him   4. drawings 5. dogs
6. logs 7. him 8. evidence 9. tools   10. date

3.8 THE POSSESSIVE CASE SHOWS OWNERSHIP.

. The possessive case of nouns and some pronouns is formed by adding an apostrophe and the letter *s* to the singular form and only an apostrophe to the plural form that ends in *s*. Here are the rules.

■ **Rule 1. To form the possessive of singular nouns, add apostrophe s.**

EXAMPLES

☐ I saw *Mary's* book on the shelf.
☐ The *horse's* mane was uncombed.
☐ The *child's* mother was asleep.

■ **The same rule applies to compound nouns; that is, to singular nouns that consist of more than one word.**

EXAMPLES

☐ The *attorney-at-law's* arguments were convincing.
☐ The *father-in-law's* hat was missing.

■ **Rule 2. To form the possessive of plural nouns that end in *s*, add only an apostrophe.**

☐ The boys' feet were cold.
☐ The pilots' directions were incorrect.

■ **Rule 3. The possessive of plural compound nouns is formed in the same way as is the possessive of singular compound nouns; that is, by adding apostrophe *s*. Note that the plural is formed by adding *s* to the first word.**

☐ The *attorneys-at-law's* arguments were convincing.
☐ The *fathers-in-law's* hats were missing.

■ **Rule 4. To form the possessive of plural nouns that do not end in *s*, add an apostrophe and *s*.**

☐ The *women's* dresses were blue.
☐ The *children's* playground was nearby.
☐ The *geese's* feathers were white.

■ There is not complete agreement regarding the possessive of singular nouns that end in the letter *s*. The possessive may be formed either by adding apostrophe and *s*, or by adding only an apostrophe.

☐ Jones's farm
or ☐ Jones' farm

☐ Agnes's dress
or ☐ Agnes' dress

The first form is usually preferred. However, the guide is usually how the possessive form sounds when it is spoken. Some authorities prefer to add only an apostrophe, not apostrophe *s*, when the noun ends with the sound of *s*, *z*, *sh*, or *zh*, especially if the word has more than one syllable.

EXAMPLES

One syllable word - add apostrophe and s.

☐ Burns's poems
☐ Marx's comedies
☐ Jones's home

More than one syllable - add only an apostrophe

☐ conscience' sake
☐ Jesus' teachings
☐ Berlioz' music

■ **If there is joint possession by two or more proper nouns, add apostrophe *s* to the last name only.**

EXAMPLES

☐ Wilson, Lewis, and Winter's law firm.
☐ May and Joy's book.

■ **But if there is individual ownership, the apostrophe and *s* is added to all names.**

EXAMPLE

☐ Janelle's and Joy's books.

FOR PRACTICE

Write both the singular possessive and the plural possessive for these words.

		Singular Possessive	*Plural Possessive*
1.	man	_____	_____
2.	army	_____	_____
3.	woman	_____	_____
4.	father	_____	_____
5.	veteran	_____	_____
6.	lady	_____	_____
7.	ox	_____	_____
8.	sailor	_____	_____
9.	goose	_____	_____
10.	lawyer	_____	_____

Then test yourself further by adding apostrophe *s* or an apostrophe to form the correct possessive in each of these sentences.

11. We found the boys ___ gloves in the car.

12. They attended a mothers-in-law ___ convention.

13. The critics ___ reviews were published yesterday.

14. He read some of John Knox ___ sermons.

15. I took a two-month ___ vacation.

16. For goodness ___ sake, let me do that!

17. It was Henry and Joe ___ guitar.

18. We visited Judge Brandeis ___ home.

19. James ___ father came to see us.

20. He was a student of Socrates ___ teachings.

ANSWERS

1. man's	men's	2. army's	armies'
3. woman's	women's	4. father's	fathers'
5. veteran's	veterans'	6. lady's	ladies'
7. ox's	oxen's	8. sailor's	sailors'
9. goose's	geese's	10. lawyer's	lawyers'
11. boys'		12. mothers-in-law's	
13. critics'		14. Knox's	
15. two-month's		16. goodness'	
17. Joe's		18. Brandeis'	
19. James's or James'		20. Socrates'	

3.9 POSSESSIVE PERSONAL PRONOUNS DO NOT NEED APOSTROPHES.

■ **Rule 1. Do not use an apostrophe with a personal pronoun.**

The reason for that rule is that personal pronouns have a special form for the possessive case that does not require apostrophes.

EXAMPLES

- ☐ He is *our* dog.
- ☐ This is *my* house.
- ☐ *Your* book is on the table.
- ☐ The pencil is *mine*.
- ☐ The book is *yours*.
- ☐ *Whose* book is this?
- ☐ *Their* car is new.
- ☐ *His* farm is large.
- ☐ The dog wagged *its* tail.
- ☐ The blouse is *hers*.

■ **Rule 2. Indefinite pronouns and reciprocal pronouns require apostrophes to show possession. The indefinite pronouns** include *each, either, any, anyone, some, someone, one, not one, few, all, everyone,* and similar pronouns. The reciprocal pronouns are *each other* and *one another.*

EXAMPLES

- □ They wore *each other's* coats.
- □ She is *everyone's* friend.
- □ *Somebody's* automobile is blocking the driveway.
- □ *No one's* name was called.

■   **Rule 3. Generally, the possessive case should be used immediately before a gerund. You recall that a gerund is a verb ending in *ing* and used as a noun.**

EXAMPLES

- □ His *talking* annoyed me.
- □ Her *playing* was beautiful.

In those sentences the words *talking* and *playing* are gerunds (verbals) used as nouns and are the subjects of the sentences. Note that the pronouns immediately in front are in the possessive case.

Whether you use the possessive case before a gerund makes a difference in the meaning. That can be illustrated with these sentences.

EXAMPLES

- □ I like Margot dancing.
- □ I like Margot's dancing.

The first sentence implies that you like Margot while she is dancing, but when she is not dancing perhaps you don't like her. The second sentence with the possessive case is much clearer in stating that it is the dancing she does that you like.

☐ I do not like his working on the railroad.
☐ I do not like him working on the railroad.

The first sentence, with the possessive pronoun, states that you disapprove of the kind of job he has. The second sentence, however, implies that you are not fond of him when he is working on the railroad, but otherwise you like him all right. The careful writer is sensitive to such nuances in meaning.

FOR PRACTICE

Underline the correct word in parentheses in each of these sentences.

1. I love to listen to (him, his) playing the piano.
2. We all visited (one anothers, one another's) homes.
3. Does the dog know (it's, its) way home.
4. (Who's, Whose) name shall I give?
5. (Someones, Someone's) coat is missing.
6. This book is (hers, her's).
7. I remember (them, their) telling us about the park.
8. Do you know (whose, who's) going with us?
9. If this coat is (your's, yours), take it with you.
10. Is this coat (theirs, their's)?

ANSWERS

1. his	2. one another's	3. its	4. Whose
5. Someone's	6. hers	7. their	8. who's
9. yours	10. theirs		

3.10   AVOID APOSTROPHE FEVER.

A distressing number of errors are made in the use of this little mark ('), which, as you know, is called the *apostrophe*. It seems that some people cannot resist using an apostrophe in any word that ends in the letter *s*.

As an example, if Mr. Wells owns a grocery, it is Wells' Grocery, not Well's Grocery. (Actually, it is better to write Wells Grocery without any apostrophe.)

As another example, it is wrong to write Big Brother's/Big Sister's Inc. The correct name of the organization is Big Brothers/Big Sisters, Inc., without the apostrophes because the words are only plural nouns, not possessive nouns.

■ **Remember that the possessive form of personal pronouns does not need apostrophes. They are already possessive.**

EXAMPLES

Correct: □ ours, his, her, theirs, its, yours
Incorrect: □ our's, ours', their', theirs', it's, its', your's, yours'

■ **Possessive nouns do need apostrophes.**

EXAMPLES

These are correct.

□ five-cents' worth
□ my father's car
□ an hour's warning
□ your heart's desire
□ at arm's length
□ a day's drive

Be sure to distinguish between possessive pronouns and contractions.

EXAMPLES

Possessive Pronouns

- □ *Whose* book is this?
- □ *Their* dinner is ready.
- □ *Your* garden is green.
- □ The wine has lost *its* flavor.

Contractions

- □ *Who's* winning the game?
  (Who is)
- □ *They're* eating dinner.
  (They are)
- □ *You're* a brave man.
  (You are)
- □ *It's* been a long time.
  (It has)

One of the most common errors is writing *it's* for *its*. *Its* is the possessive pronoun; *it's* is a contraction meaning *it is*.

EXAMPLES

Correct: □ The doll had lost *its* arm.
            (possessive pronoun)
Correct: □ *It's* a pretty doll.
            (It is a pretty doll.)

■ **The apostrophe has other uses besides showing possession. It is also used to show contractions and the plurals of letters and numbers. A contraction is two words written as one, with an apostrophe showing where a letter, letters, or numbers are left out.**

1. Letters omitted

    □ I'm — I am
    □ he's —he is
    □ they're — they are
    □ who's — who is
    □ can't — cannot

2. Numbers omitted

    □ '85 Ferrari
    □ Class of '72
    □ Blizzard of '77

■ **The apostrophe is used to form the plural of letters and numbers.**

EXAMPLES

    □ She wrote her *ABC's* neatly.
    □ Cross your *t's* and dot your *i's*.
    □ The Depression was during the *1930's*.

Note: It is incorrect to form a regular plural by adding an apostrophe *s*, but it is correct to form the plural of numbers and letters by adding apostrophe *s*. This is one of the most common errors.

EXAMPLES

Correct: □ Don't lose your books.
Incorrect: □ Don't lose your book's.

Correct: □ He didn't pronounce his h's.
Incorrect: □ He didn't pronounce his hs.

FOR PRACTICE

Underline the correct form in the parentheses in these sentences.

1. (He's, Hes') our oldest son.
2. She attended the (ladies', ladie's) luncheon.
3. The bird fluttered (its, it's) wings.
4. (It's, Its) a beautiful song.
5. He is on a (three weeks, three-weeks') vacation.
6. (It's, Its) been three days since I have seen him.
7. Is this book (yours, your's)?
8. Mike attends meetings of a (men's, mens') club in the city.
9. I know (who's, whose) coming to dinner.
10. That land is (ours, ours').

ANSWERS

1. He's	2. ladies'	3. its	4. It's
5. three-weeks'	6. It's	7. yours	8. men's
9. who's	10. ours		

TEST ON CASE

In each of these sentences underline the correct pronoun in parentheses and write the letter from this list in the blank to indicate why your answer is correct.

A. Subject of a verb
B. Predicate nominative
C. Object of the infinitive to be which has no subject

D. Direct object of a verb
E. Indirect object of a verb
F. Object of a preposition
G. Subject of an infinitive
H. Object of an infinitive
I. Possessive in front of a gerund

1. __ All of (us, we) members of the team were ready to play.

2. __ It was (she, her) who told us the news.

3. __ If it were to be (them, they) who are chosen, I would be happy.

4. __ I heard about (you, your) winning a prize for the best roses.

5. __ He asked (who, whom) to help do the work?

6. __ She is the kind of nurse (who, whom) they thought would take good care of our mother.

7. __ The company hired my father and (I, me) to work the night shift.

8. __ Susan did not want Jolene and (she, her) to learn the secret.

9. __ (Who, Whom) are you looking for?

10. __ Yesterday the teacher praised Tom and (I, me) for our good work.

11. __ Mr. Wilson is pleased with a pupil named Jones, (who, whom) he knows will always have his lessons well prepared.

12. __ I did not want to follow Mary or (she, her).

13. __ Will you call Margie and (I, me) some day next week?

14. __ The teacher wanted Henry to tell Louise and (I, me) the answer to the question.

15. __ She was worried about her (mother, mother's) getting home safely.

16. __ I wouldn't want to be (he, him).

17. __ They wanted Nancy and (I, me) to start first.

18. __ I hope you don't mind (me, my) stopping by.

19. __ (Who, Whom) do you think him to be?

20. __ (Who, Whom) are the officials we want to question?

21. __ He is supposed to be (who, whom)?

22. __ Martin believed it would be (he, him) who would be elected.

23. __ (Who, Whom) were they expecting to answer the telephone?

24. __ Aunt Lily gave Janice and (I, me) a box of candy.

25. __ When I was young, my father gave my brother and (I, me) a little red wagon.

Write the possessive of these nouns and pronouns.

26. man _____   31. each other _____
27. men _____   32. person _____
28. John _____   33. brother-in-law _____
29. everyone _____   34. yours _____
30. engineers _____   35. Adams _____

Change these phrases to possessive form, in this manner:

☐ the birthdays of the saints   the saint's birthdays

36. the riders of the horses   _____

37. the thoughts of the mothers-in-law   _____

38. the house of the Mitchells   _____

39. the flowers of the bridesmaids   _____

40. the song of Irving Berlin   _____

41. the poems of Dorothy Parker   _____

42. worth a nickel   _____

43. worked for a day   _____

44. the noise of the machine   _____

45. the policy of the United States   _____

ANSWERS

1. F - *us*, object of the preposition *of*.
2. B - *she*, predicate nominative (It was *she*).
3. C - *they*, object of the infinitive *to be* which has no subject.
4. I - *your*, possessive before gerund *winning*.
5. G - *whom*, subject of the infinitive *to help*.
6. A - *who*, subject of the verb *would take*.
7. D - *me*, direct object of the verb *hired*.
8. G - *her*, subject of the infinitive *to learn*.
9. F - *Whom*, object of the preposition *for*.
10. D - *me*, object of the verb *praised*.
11. A - *who*, subject of the verb *will have*.
12. H - *her*, object of the infinitive *to follow*.
13. D - *me*, object of the verb *will call*.
14. H - *me*, object of the infinitive *to tell*.
15. I - *mother's*, possessive before the gerund *getting*.
16. C - *he*, object of the infinitive *to be* which has no subject.
17. G - *me*, subject of the infinitive *to start*.
18. I - *my*, possessive before the gerund *stopping*.
19. H - *Whom*, object of the infinitive *to be* which has a subject.
20. A - *Who*, subject of the verb *are*.
21. C - *who*, object of the infinitive *to be* which has no subject.
22. B - *he*, predicate nominative (it would be he).
23. G - *Whom*, subject of the infinitive *to answer*.
24. E - *me*, indirect object of the verb *gave*.
25. E - *me*, indirect object of the verb *gave*.
26. man's
27. men's
28. John's
29. everyone's
30. engineers'
31. each other's
32. person's
33. brother-in-law's
34. yours
35. Adams'
36. horses' riders
37. mothers-in-law's
38. Mitchells' house
39. bridesmaids' flowers
40. Irving Berlin's songs
41. Dorothy Parker's poems
42. nickel's worth
43. day's work
44. machine's noise
45. United States' policy

4

MODIFIERS

As has been said before, the subject and the verb are the essential parts of every sentence. Anything else included or added to the sentence tells about either the subject or the verb. The "anything else" that is added is called a *modifier*. It explains, describes, and limits the word or words it modifies.

A modifier may be a word (an adjective or an adverb), or it may be a phrase (two or more related words that have no subject or verb), or it may be a dependent clause. There may be several different modifiers in a single sentence.

4.1 ADJECTIVES AND ADVERBS ARE MODIFIERS.

■ A *modifier* is a word or group of words that describes or explains (modifies) another word or group of words. Modifiers add information to the sentence.

There are several kinds of modifiers. Among them are adjectives and adverbs. You learned about them in the section on parts of speech. Here is a brief review.

Adjectives

Adjectives modify nouns and pronouns, as you learned in Lesson 2.12. To repeat from that lesson, suppose you write *men*. Then when you write *tall men*, you have used the adjective *tall* to modify the noun *men*. You have limited the noun to only *tall men*.

EXAMPLES

- □ a *sudden* change
- □ a *violent* storm
- □ a *white* house

You can see in those examples that the adjective precedes the noun it modifies; that is, it is immediately in front of the noun. But that is not always true. You recall studying predicate complements in Lesson 2.22 where you learned that the predicate adjective comes after a linking verb.

EXAMPLES

- □ She is *pretty*.
- □ The milk is *sour*.
- □ He felt *ill*.

In each of those sentences, the adjective in the predicate describes (modifies) the subject, which is either a noun or a pronoun.

Adverbs

Adverbs are not quite as simple as adjectives because, as you learned in Lesson 2.14, they modify verbs, adverbs, and adjectives.

EXAMPLES

☐ He ran *swiftly*.
(Here *swiftly* is an adverb that modifies the verb *ran*. It tells how he ran.)

☐ He ran *more* swiftly than I.
(Here the word *more* is an adverb that modifies the adverb *swiftly*.)

☐ She was a *very* tired woman.
(Here the word *very* is an adverb that modifies the adjective *tired* which modifies the noun *woman*.)

FOR PRACTICE

To be sure you can distinguish between the two, write in the blank whether the italicized word in the sentence is an adjective or an adverb.

1. They *soon* came home.   _____

2. He came *directly* to the house.   _____

3. There was a *sudden* change in the weather.   _____

4. The weather changed *suddenly*.   _____

5. He played *well* at defensive end.   _____

6. Ruth felt *happy*.   _____

7. Mary felt the cloth *carefully*.   _____

8. She tied the string *tightly*.   _____

9. He walked a *tight* rope.   _____

10. He came *upstairs*.   _____

Next, underline the noun or pronoun that each of the italicized adjectives modify.

11. The noise was *loud*.
12. He lives in a *distant* country.
13. Willie was an *early* riser.
14. She has *little* energy.
15. *Most* people went home.

Then underline the words that these adverbs modify.

16. Drive *slowly* down the road.
17. She arrived *late*.
18. He lived *high* on the mountain.
19. Do it *right* the first time.
20. He swam *rapidly*.

ANSWERS

1. adverb	2. adverb	3. adjective	4. adverb
5. adverb	6. adjective	7. adverb	8. adverb
9. adjective	10. adverb	11. noise	12. country
13. riser	14. energy	15. people	16. Drive
17. arrived	18. lived	19. Do	20. swam

4.2 SOME BUT NOT ALL PHRASES ARE MODIFIERS.

You have already learned that a phrase is a group of two or more grammatically related words that has no subject or predicate and that functions as a single part of speech.

■ **A *noun phrase* consists of a noun and its modifiers.**

EXAMPLES

☐ The *old man* entered the room.
☐ He told us a *long story*.

In the first sentence the noun phrase is the subject of the verb *entered*; in the second sentence the phrase is the object of the verb *told*.

■ **A *verb phrase* is simply a verb plus its helping (auxiliary) verbs.**

EXAMPLE

☐ I *would have written* to you had I known your address.

Those two kinds of phrases, noun and verb, are relatively simple and need be of little concern.   There are, however, other kinds of phrases that deserve more study.

Prepositional Phrases

You learned in Lesson 2.17 that a prepositional phrase is a group of two or more words that begin with a preposition and usually end with a noun or a pronoun. A prepositional phrase may function as a noun or as an adjective or as an adverb.

EXAMPLES

Noun phrase: ☐ *Behind the barn* is the location of the well.
(The phrase, the subject of the sentence, serves as a noun.)

Adverb phrase: □   He walked *into the garden*.
(The phrase serves as an adverb, modifying the verb *walked* by telling where he walked.)

Adjective phrase:□   He has a garden *of beautiful flowers*.
(The phrase serves as an adjective, modifying the noun *garden*.)

Infinitive Phrases

An infinitive, you recall, is a verb with the word *to* in front of it. Examples are *to go, to run, to hope, to be, to win,* or in the perfect tense, *to have gone, to have run, to have hoped, to have been,* and *to have won.* The word *to* used in this fashion is called "the sign of the infinitive."

■   **When you add one or more words to an infinitive, you have written an infinitive phrase. An infinitive phrase may function as a noun or an adjective or an adverb.**

EXAMPLES

As a noun, subject of the verb *is*:
□   *To succeed as an accountant* is my goal.

As a noun, object of the verb *like*:
□   We like *to eat fresh fruit*.

As a noun, object of the preposition *except*:
□   We never stopped working *except to rest now and then*.

As an adjective modifying the noun *movie*:
□   The movie t*o be shown at noon* is about life in China.

As an adverb, modifying the verb *went*:
□   We went *to help with the work*.

Gerund Phrases

A gerund, you recall, is a verb that ends in *ing* and is used as a noun. A noun, you also recall, may be the subject of a sentence (subject of a verb), the direct or the indirect object of a verb, the predicate nominative, or the object of a preposition. A word used as a noun is never a modifier; thus gerunds and gerund phrases are not modifiers.

Subject of the sentence: □ *Attending college* is expensive.

Object of the verb *enjoyed*: □ I enjoyed *operating the computer*.

Object of the preposition *except*: □ We enjoyed all the work *except filing reports*.

Participial Phrases

When you studied the tense of verbs, you learned that two forms of verbs are called participles. One is the present participle, which ends in *ing*; the other is the past participle, many but not all of which end in *ed*.

Present Participle: □ *walking*
Past Participle: □ *walked*

■ **Add one or more words to a participle and you have a participial phrase. Participial phrases that begin with the present participles and gerund phrases that begin with gerunds look alike because they both begin with verbs that end in *ing*. The difference in their use is that a gerund is always used as a noun and a participle is used as an adjective.**

Present participles used as adjectives: □ *dancing* waves
     □ *moving* truck

Past participles | ☐ *wounded* animal
used as adjectives: | ☐ *educated* people

EXAMPLES

- ☐ *Tired of waiting*, they went home.
- ☐ *Waiting for two hours*, Maxwell became tired.
- ☐ He saw the book *lying on the table*.

The participial phrase in the first sentence modifies *they*; in the second sentence, the phrase modifies Maxwell; and in the third sentence, the participial phrase modifies *book*. In each of the three sentences the participial phrase serves as an adjective by modifying a noun.

Absolute Phrases

■ **An absolute phrase doesn't function as a part of speech; rather, it modifies the entire main clause.**

EXAMPLES

- ☐ *The guests having arrived*, we served dinner.
- ☐ *The storm over*, Glen set out for home.
- ☐ *The sun now above the horizon*, we began our journey.

FOR PRACTICE

The prepositional phrases in these sentences are in italics. To test yourself, underline the word in each sentence that the phrase modifies.

1. He walked *around the room.*
2. The door *at the front* was red.
3. The fruit *in that jar* is spoiled.
4. He picked a dozen roses *from the vine.*

5. The flowers grew abundantly *in the window box.*

6. The man *in the garden* was working.

7. The man was working *in the garden.*

8. The program *on television last night* was hilarious.

9. Many *of the members* were absent.

10. Bernie plunged *into the pool.*

Underline the phrase in each of these sentences.

11. *Gerund phrase.* Taking an ocean cruise is very enjoyable.

12. *Noun phrase.* A sumptuous meal was ready for us.

13. *Verb phrase.* That rule has been abolished.

14. *Infinitive phrase.* We went t*o* see a movie.

15. *Participial phrase.* Stopped by the barricade, we didn't know where to go.

16. *Participial phrase.* Working long hours, William became discouraged.

17. *Absolute phrase.* The hour having arrived, we began our journey.

18. *Appositive phrase.* Our teacher, a brilliant mathematician, was absent that day.

19. *Prepositional phrase.* She works in the garden.

20. *Infinitive phrase.* We wanted to help her.

ANSWERS

1. walked	2. door	3. fruit	4. picked
5. grew	6. man	7. was working	8. program
9. Many	10. plunged	11. Taking an ocean cruise	
12. A sumptuous meal		13. has been abolished	
14. to see a movie		15. Stopped by the barricade	

16. Working long hours   17. The hour having arrived
18. a brilliant mathematician 19. in the garden
20. to help her

4.3 ADJECTIVE AND ADVERB CLAUSES ARE MODIFIERS.

Dependent (subordinate) clauses also function as parts of speech. A dependent clause may serve as a noun, as an adjective, or as an adverb.

■ **Dependent clauses that serve as nouns begin with the words** *whether, when, where, why, how* **or a relative pronoun. Relative pronouns, which introduce dependent clauses, are listed in Lesson 1.11. Among them are** *who, whom, which, that.*

EXAMPLES

□ *What he said* angered us.
□ *How he came out of that accident alive* is a mystery.

The dependent clause in each of those sentences is the subject of the sentence and thus functions as a noun.

□ I'll never know *how he came out of that accident alive.*
□ I will give him *whichever book he wants.*

The dependent clauses in those sentences are objects of verbs and thus function as nouns.

□ I want to know *who is coming to the reception.*

The dependent clause in that sentence is the object of the infinitive *to know*, also functioning as a noun.

■   **Dependent clauses that serve as adjectives begin with relative pronouns.**

   □   The Alamo, *which is in Texas*, is a tourist attraction.
   □   The dog *that won the prize* is a Dalmatian.
   □   Jason, *who retrieved the Golden Fleece*, was the leader of the Argonauts.

In the first sentence, the adjective clause modifies the noun, *The Alamo*; in the second, the clause modifies *The dog*; and in the third, it modifies *Jason*. In all three sentences the nouns modified by the adjective clauses are the subjects of the sentences.

■   **Dependent clauses that serve as adverbs begin with subordinating conjunctions. Among the subordinating conjunctions, which connect dependent clauses to independent clauses to form complex sentences, are *if, since, because, when, before, after*. Others are listed in Lesson 1.11.**

   □   We will leave *before the sun sets*.
   □   *When we told him about the prize*, he was happy.
   □   He went to bed *after he ate supper*.

In the first sentence, the adverb clause modifies the verb *will leave*. In the second sentence, the adverb clause modifies the predicate adjective *happy*; and in the third sentence, the adverb clause modifies the verb *went*.

■   **Adverb phrases and clauses function as modifiers by telling how, when, where, why, and how much.**

EXAMPLES

The adverbs and adverb clauses and phrases are italicized.

How:
- □ He spoke *loudly*.
- □ He spoke *in a loud voice*.

When:
- □ He will arrive *soon*.
- □ He will arrive *in the morning*.
- □ He arrived *after the sun had set*.

Where:
- □ He worked *in the garden*.
- □ He worked *wherever he wanted to*.

Why:
- □ He worked *because he needed the money*.

How Much:
- □ This juice is *too* bitter to drink.
- □ He worked *until he was exhausted*.

FOR PRACTICE

In the blank, write whether the subordinate clause is an adverb or an adjective. There are five of each.

1. While he was in the kitchen, I ran outdoors and Denise went with me. _____

2. If I had some money, I would buy a book. _____

3. The story, which I believed, was very strange. _____

4. Although it was raining, he continued to work in the garden. _____

5. The speaker who people thought was Irish was actually Welsh. _____

6. The man who bought our house is a lawyer. _____

7. When she comes home in March, we will have a celebration. _____

8. Marie read a book while I washed dishes. _____

9. The city of Fairbanks, which is near the Arctic Circle, is very cold in winter. _____

10. The flowers that filled the garden were beautiful. _____

Next, underline the word or words each subordinate clause modifies.

11. Unless you study, you will not learn the language.

12. I smiled at him, although I was angry.

13. Ocean perch, which is delicious, is one of my favorite foods.

14. The man who gave me this pencil is my teacher.

15. My dog, which I like very much, is a Dalmatian.

16. The man that stopped us is a policeman.

17. I waited until he arrived.

18. She talked with him after he had won the election.

19. This is the house that Jack built.

20. I haven't seen him since we were together at Easter time.

ANSWERS

1. adverb	2. adverb	3. adjective	4. adverb
5. adjective	6. adjective	7. adverb	8. adverb
9. adjective	10. adjective	11. will learn	12. smiled
13. perch	14. man	15. dog	16. man
17. waited	18. talked	19. house	20. have seen

4.4 APPOSITIVES ARE MODIFIERS.

■   An *appositive* is a noun or noun phrase that helps to identify the noun or pronoun that it follows. An appositive may consist of one or more words, and it does not have a subject or a verb.

☐ Andrew, *the chairman*, called the meeting to order.

Here is a sentence that has two subjects, both in italics.

☐ *Cheryl* and *Jennifer* are pretty girls.

Now suppose one or more words are added to describe or tell about the girls. It could read this way, with the appositives in italics.

☐ Cheryl, *the younger girl*, and Jennifer, *the older girl*, are both beautiful.

■ **Appositives are modifiers. They help to explain or identify the noun or pronoun just before or after them. Note that an appositive is usually separated from the rest of the sentence by commas, with a comma in front and a comma at the end. An appositive usually follows the word or words it modifies, but it can come before.**

EXAMPLE

☐ *A well-educated woman*, Sandra could speak eloquently.

When the appositive precedes the word or words it modifies, only one comma is needed.

When only one or two words form an appositive and they are closely related to the subject, commas are not needed.

EXAMPLES

☐ Our daughter *Susan* attended Oberlin College.
☐ His dog *Tige* ran after the rabbit.

As stated previously, the use of commas makes a difference in the meaning of the sentence. The meaning is not quite the same when commas are used. This sentence will illustrate.

EXAMPLES

- ☐   The beautiful girl Marjorie won the prize.
- ☐   The beautiful girl, Marjorie, won the prize.

The first sentence, without the commas, is merely a statement of fact. The second sentence, however, with the commas, implies or suggests that there was one or more girls besides Marjorie but that Marjorie was the beautiful one and the other girl or girls were not beautiful.

■   **An appositive is in the same case as the word or words it identifies. This was mentioned in Lesson 3.2.**

EXAMPLES

- ☐   Bill Engle, *a sportscaster*, was one of those honored at the banquet.
- ☐   We saw Henry, *our neighbor*, at the fair.
- ☐   He objected to the nomination of John, *the auditor*.

In the first sentence, the appositive, *a sportscaster*, is in the nominative case, as is Bill Engle, the subject of the sentence. In the second sentence, the word *Henry* is in the objective case as the object of the verb *saw* and thus the appositive *neighbor* is in the objective case. In the third sentence, *John* is in the objective case as the object of the preposition *of*, so the appositive *auditor* is in the objective case.

■   **Rule. Separate an appositive from the rest of the sentence with commas, except when the subject and the appositive are very closely related and brief.**

FOR PRACTICE

Underline the appositives in these sentences.

1. Antonio, the butcher, is friendly.
2. Edgar, a fast-talking salesman, works at Sears.
3. Caroline, a cheerful and amusing girl, told us a story.
4. Dr. Wilson, our family physician, bandaged my wrist.
5. A prolific songwriter, Irving Berlin died September 22, 1989.

Punctuate these sentences with commas.

6. The wedding a formal affair was held in the church.
7. The child a six-year-old girl went home with us.
8. The bird an ivory billed woodpecker suddenly flew away.
9. Monday July 6 is my birthday.
10. Captain Long an officer in the Air Force is home on a visit.

ANSWERS

1. the butcher   2. a fast-talking salesman
3. a cheerful and amusing girl   4. our family physician
5. A prolific songwriter
6. The wedding, a formal affair, was held in the church.
7. The child, a six-year-old girl, went home with us.
8. The bird, an ivory billed woodpecker, suddenly flew away.
9. Monday, July 6, is my birthday.
10. Captain Long, an officer in the Air Force, is home on a visit.

4.5 MISPLACED MODIFIERS CAN BE MISLEADING.

Note that the location of the italicized modifying phrases gives unintended meanings to these sentences.

EXAMPLES

- ☐ The pathologist decided that the man died of heart failure *after an autopsy.*
- ☐ Samuel Hines was fined for drunken driving *in municipal court* this morning.

A misplaced adverb can give an unintended meaning to a sentence.

EXAMPLE

- ☐ The court has sentenced him to die *twice.*

Obviously, a person doesn't die twice, or even once after an autopsy, or drive while drunk in municipal court. Placement of the modifiers make enormous differences in the meaning of sentences.

■ **Rule. Place modifiers as closely as possible to the word or words they modify.**

In the sentences above, *after an autopsy* should follow the verb *decided*; *in municipal court should* follow the verb *was fined*; and *twice* should modify *sentenced.* The sentences would then read as follows:

- ☐ The pathologist decided *after an autopsy* that the man died of heart failure.
- ☐ Samuel Hines was fined *in municipal court* this morning for drunken driving.
- ☐ The court has *twice* sentenced him to die.

How placement affects meaning can be illustrated with the adverb *only*, as discussed in Lesson 2.15.

- □   *Only* I love Monique.
- □   I love *only* Monique.

The first sentence means that I am the only person who loves Monique. The second sentence means that she is the only person I love.

- □   He said *yesterday* that the fire resulted from faulty wiring.
- □   He said that the fire *yesterday* resulted from faulty wiring.

The first sentence tells when he said it; the second tells when the fire occurred. The difference in meaning results from the change of the word *yesterday* from one location in the sentence to another.

A common error occurs in misplacing prepositional phrases and other modifiers that tell when and where. Here is an example of a misplaced prepositional phrase.

- □   Joe Doakes was sentenced to six months in the county jail for assaulting Henry James *in the circuit court yesterday*.

Obviously the assault did not take place in the court yesterday. It was the sentencing that took place in the court yesterday, so the sentence should read as follows:

- □   Joe Doakes was sentenced *in the circuit court yesterday* to six months in the county jail for assaulting Henry James.

Here is another example of a misplaced modifier.

□   The Lybarger-Grimm Auxiliary was awarded a ribbon for meeting the membership quota for five consecutive years *at the Department Convention in Columbus last weekend.*

As worded, the sentence states that the five-year quota was met at the Convention last weekend, which was, of course, impossible. It takes five years to meet a five-year quota; but recognition for meeting the quota can be given on a weekend. The sentence should read this way:

□   The Lybarger-Grimm Auxiliary was awarded a ribbon *at the Department Convention in Columbus last weekend* for meeting the membership quota for five consecutive years.

■   **A modifier is said to *dangle* when it fails to refer to a particular noun or pronoun or when the word it modifies is not the word intended.**

The dangling modifiers in these sentences are in italics:

□   *Upon reaching the house*, his burden seemed lighter.

In that sentence the modifying phrase seems to refer to *his burden*. It can be rewritten as follows:
□   When he reached the house, his burden seemed lighter.

□   *To learn grammar*, the textbook must be easy to read.

The infinitive phrase in that sentence refers to *textbook*, which is not what the writer intended. The sentence seems to say that the textbook is learning grammar. Instead, the sentence might read:

☐ To learn grammar, a student needs a textbook that is easy to read.

☐ *While walking in the garden,* Jason arrived.

That sentence does not make clear who was walking in the garden. It may be written in this manner.

☐ While I was walking in the garden, Jason arrived.

■ **It is important to note that a participial phrase at the beginning of a sentence always modifies (tells something about) the first word (the subject) of the main clause. It is here that errors commonly occur.**

These sentences illustrate such errors.

EXAMPLES

☐ *Resting on a bench in the park,* the journey seemed long and tiresome.
☐ *Having taken our seats,* the show began immediately.

The first sentence seems to say that the journey was resting on a bench, and the second sentence seems to say that the show had taken our seats.

In grammar, a participial phrase such as those is said to *dangle.* The meaning is not clear in sentences that have dangling participles. The two sentences could be rewritten this way.

☐ Resting on a bench in the park, we thought our journey had been long and tiresome.
☐ Immediately after we took our seats, the show began.

Here is another example of a dangling phrase.

☐ *The man was accused of stealing the automobile,* wearing a black leather coat.

In that sentence, the participial phrase belongs after *man*, not after *automobile*, for the meaning to be clear.

☐   The man wearing a black leather coat was accused of stealing the automobile.

FOR PRACTICE

Rewrite these sentences to make the meaning clear.

1. Tired of working, retirement is the best solution.

    ☐ _____

2. While studying grammar, the telephone rang.

    ☐ _____

3. Taking the bus, the driver helped us to reach our destination.

    ☐ _____

4. Buying a large quantity, the merchant gave us a rebate.

    ☐ _____

5. After leaving for home, the car ran out of gasoline.

    ☐ _____

ANSWERS

Among the several ways those sentences may be restated, these are suggested.

1. For anyone tired of working, retirement is the best solution.
2. While he was studying grammar, the telephone rang.
3. We took the bus, and the driver helped us to reach our destination.
4. Because we bought a large quantity, the merchant gave us a rebate.
5. After we left for home, the car ran out of gasoline.

4.6 PARENTHETICAL EXPRESSIONS ARE SET OFF BY COMMAS.

■ *A parenthetical expression* is a word or words that interrupt, but unlike an appositive, it does not explain or modify.

EXAMPLES

- □ *Yes*, I want some.
- □ *No*, I do not know him.
- □ *Well*, I want to go home now.
- □ He mentioned, *for example*, a change in the date of the event.
- □ It's a dark night, *isn't it*?

Note that parenthetical expressions are not essential to the meaning or construction of the sentence. In that respect, they are akin to such elements as appositives, descriptive phrases, nonrestrictive clauses, and forms of direct address which are non-essential but do add information.

And like other non-essential elements, parenthetical expressions are separated from the rest of the sentence with commas. That is important to remember because the addition or omission of a comma can and frequently does change the meaning of a sentence. That fact is illustrated in the punctuation of a direct address, as explained in Lesson 1.13, but repeated here.

EXAMPLES

- □ Norman, the farmer went to town.
- □ Norman, the farmer, went to town.

The first sentence is an example of direct address. *Norman* is addressed and told that the farmer went to town. The addition of a comma after *farmer* in the second sentence changes the meaning completely. The words, *the farmer*, become an appositive identifying *Norman*.

The first sentence says that the farmer but not Norman went to town; the second says that Norman the farmer went to town.

The use of commas to set off nonrestrictive clauses is not only critical for the writer to convey his meaning, as explained in Lesson 1.13, but it aids the reader. Note how much easier it is to read the second sentence here, in which the nonrestrictive clause is set off completely by commas, than it is the first sentence which has only one comma.

EXAMPLES

- ☐ William Ulrich, who is chairman of the company was born and reared in Boston.
- ☐ William Ulrich, who is chairman of the company, was born and reared in Boston.

FOR PRACTICE

Place commas as needed in these sentences.

1. A right angle which has 90 degrees is what he is trying to draw.
2. Louise a primary school teacher writes children's poetry.
3. I told Gretchen to read the lesson.
4. He said Mary you should read the lesson.
5. Read one of your poems aloud Milton.
6. He is I understand a learned man.
7. I want you by all means to come with me.
8. Hey come here.
9. I wonder what he is doing now.
10. He said yes he would come.
11. Norman who went to school with me is now a doctor.

ANSWERS

1. A right angle, which has 90 degrees, is what he is trying to draw.
2. Louise, a primary school teacher, writes children's poetry.
3. I told Gretchen to read the lesson.
4. He said, Mary, you should read the lesson.
5. Read one of your poems aloud, Milton.
6. He is, I understand, a learned man.
7. I want you, by all means, to come with me.
8. Hey, come here.
9. I wonder what he is doing now.
10. He said, yes, he would come.
11. Norman, who went to school with me, is now a doctor.

REVIEW OF MODIFIERS

■ A modifier is a word or a group of words that describes or explains (modifies) another word or group of words. Adjectives modify nouns and pronouns; adverbs modify verbs, adjectives, and other adverbs.

To see how well you recognize adjectives and adverbs and what they modify, write in the blank whether the italicized word in the sentence is an adjective or an adverb. Then carry it further by underlining the word the adjective or adverb modifies.

EXAMPLE

□ Walk *rapidly* to the door.   Adverb

1. The meat should be cooked *slowly*.   _____

2. It can be cooked over a *slow* fire.   _____

3. Mr. Nguyen's parents live in *faraway* Southeast Asia.   _____

4. I can come to see you *almost* any day next week.   _____

5. I can come to see you almost *any* day next week.   _____

6. Tonya answered the questions *correctly*.   _____

7. Few students knew the *correct* answer.   _____

8. We visited a *deserted* village in Wyoming.   _____

9. Andre is a *French* musician who lives in Paris.   _____

10. The team played *well* today.   _____

When choosing between the use of an adjective and an adverb, remember that if the word modifies a noun or a pronoun, use an adjective; if it modifies a verb, an adjective, or another adverb, use an adverb. It is necessary, therefore, to be able to determine what word is being modified and what part of speech it is. Test yourself further by underlining the correct word in parentheses in these sentences.

11. He played (bad, badly).

12. We won the game (easy, easily).

13. This box is (squarer, more nearly square) than that one.

14. I thought (sure, surely) he would like to read that book.

15. John is the (wealthier, wealthiest) of the two men.

16. Mary felt (happy, happily).

17. She went (happy, happily) to the picnic.

18. The coach looked (angry, angrily) at him.

19. Kevin was the (taller, tallest) man on the team.

20. He was able to play (good, well) the next day.

Not only adjectives and adverbs are modifiers, but also some phrases are modifiers. See if you can underline correctly the word the phrase in each of these sentence modifies.

21. *Prepositional phrase*: She walked around the garden.

22. *Prepositional phrase*: He has a handful of flowers.

23. *Infinitive phrase*: We like to work in the garden.

24. *Participial phrase*: We watched her working in the garden.

25. *Prepositional phrase*: The flowers in the garden are beautiful.

Dependent clauses are modifiers. Underline the word that the italicized clause in each sentence modifies.

26. She is a woman *who loves to play bridge*.

27. I will come *if you want me to*.

28. He felt better *after he had eaten supper*.

29. Carmen was happy *because she had received a high grade*.

30. That man, *whose horse won the race*, is wealthy.

Each of these sentences contains an appositive. Punctuate them correctly with commas.

31. Andrew Brown president of the Rotary Club made the announcement.

32. Malawi a country in Africa has about the same area as Pennsylvania.

33. Yolanda our neighbor does beautiful needlework.

34. Samuel L. Clemens, author of *Tom Sawyer* is known as Mark Twain.

35. An able leader Franklin D. Roosevelt was elected to four terms as president of the United States.

ANSWERS

1. adverb - cooked	2. adjective - fire
3. adjective - Southeast Asia	4. adverb - any
5. adjective - day	6. adverb - answered
7. adjective - correct	8. adjective - village
9. adjective - musician	10. adverb - played

11. badly   12. easily   13. more nearly square
14. surely   15. wealthier   16. happy
17. happily   18. angrily   19. tallest
20. well   21. walked   22. handful
23. like   24. her   25. flowers
26. woman   27. will come   28. better
29. happy   30. man

31. Andrew Brown, president of the Rotary Club, made the announcement.
32. Malawi, a country in Africa, has about the same area as Pennsylvania.
33. Yolanda, our neighbor, does beautiful needlework.
34. Samuel L. Clemens, author of *Tom Sawyer,* is known as Mark Twain.
35. An able leader, Franklin D. Roosevelt was elected to four terms as president of the United States.

AGREEMENT

Subjects and verbs must agree in number and person, and pronouns must agree with their antecedents in person, number, and gender.

5.1 VERBS MUST AGREE WITH THEIR SUBJECTS.

■ **Rule: Singular subjects take singular verbs and plural subjects take plural verbs.**

That rule can be confusing because we so often think of adding the letter *s* to form plurals, but the singular form of many verbs ends in *s* and the plural form of many nouns ends in *s*.

EXAMPLES

Singular subject:	□	A bird *flies*.
	□	The condition *permits*.
Plural subject:	□	Birds *fly*.
	□	Conditions *permit*.

You have learned that every verb has a subject, and being able to determine the subject of the verb and whether it is singular or plural is necessary for selecting the correct form of the verb. Determining the subject of a verb is not always easy, especially when the subject and the verb are separated by a phrase or a clause.

EXAMPLES

□ My *uncle*, who is a retired banker, *collects* stamps.
(My uncle collects stamps.)

□ The *problem* of raising funds to clean the lake, as well as finding workmen to do the job, *was discussed* at the meeting.
(The problem was discussed.)

□ The first *runner* across the finish line *wins* the race.
(The first runner wins the race.)

□ The *horses* in that barren land *run* wild.
(The horses run wild.)

In the last two sentences above, the subjects are separated from the verbs by prepositional phrases. Note that the noun in a prepositional phrase does not govern the verb. For example, in the last sentence above, the subject of the verb is *horses* (horses run), not *land*.

An exception to that rule occurs, however, in the use of fractions where the verb agrees with the noun in the prepositional phrase.

EXAMPLES

- About a fourth of the *trees were* damaged.
- About a fourth of the *tree was* damaged.

- Half of my *money goes* for rent.
- Half of my *dollars go* for rent.

In the first pair of sentences above, the subject is *fourth*, but the verbs are governed by the nouns in the prepositional phrases, *of the trees* and *of the tree*. In the second pair, the subject is *Half*, but the verbs are governed by the nouns in the prepositional phrases where *money* is a singular noun in the first sentence and *dollars* is a plural noun in the second sentence.

The correct verb to use depends upon the meaning of the sentence. That is also true with such words as *some*, *any*, *none*, and *all* when they are used as the subjects of sentences.

EXAMPLES

Singular: ☐ Some of the *leaf was* discolored.
Plural: ☐ Some of the *leaves were* discolored.

Singular: ☐ None of the *book was* interesting.
Plural: ☐ None of the *books were* interesting.

Singular: ☐ All of the *banana was* rotten.
Plural: ☐ All of the *bananas were* rotten.

■ **Such terms of quantity as fifty dollars, ten pounds, majority, two thirds, and number are singular when they refer to a single group or unit and plural when they refer to separate members or items.**

Singular: □   Fifty dollars *was* a high price to pay.
Plural: □   Fifty dollars *were* divided among those present.

Sometimes it is difficult to determine the subject when the subject comes after the verb.

□   I read yesterday that there *are soldiers* training for guerrilla warfare on that island.
(soldiers are training.)

□   Most disappointed of all *were the players* on the team.
(the players were disappointed)

Collective nouns can be a problem because they can be either singular or plural, depending upon the way they are used. Examples of collective nouns are class, committee, council, family, congregation, audience.

■   **When a collective noun is used to mean a single group or unit, it takes a singular verb; but when it refers to the individual members of the groups or the items in the unit, it takes a plural verb.**

□   The committee *has adjourned* for the day.
(a single group, singular verb)

□   The committee *have gone* to their offices.
(individual members, plural verb)

Indefinite pronouns, listed in Lesson 2.4 and discussed again in Lesson 5.3, do not refer to specific persons or things. They can present problems in agreement because some are always singular, some are always plural, and some may be either singular or plural.

■   The indefinite pronouns *one, anyone, everyone, someone, no one, everybody, somebody, anybody, nobody, either,* and *neither* are always singular and take a singular verb when they are subjects.

EXAMPLES

- □   *Somebody* in that group *is* missing.
- □   *Nobody was* there when it happened.
- □   *Neither* Fred nor James *was* on duty.

■   The indefinite pronouns *many, few, both,* and *several* always take plural verbs when they are subjects.

EXAMPLES

- □   *Several* of the cows *were* in the barn.
- □   *Both* boys *were* alone at home.
- □   *Few have* any money.

FOR PRACTICE

Before proceeding further in the study of agreement of verbs with their subjects, test yourself by underlining the correct verbs in the parentheses in these sentences.

1. The plate of cookies (look, looks) inviting.

2. The schedule of classes (is, are) posted on the bulletin board.

3. Many of those old jokes still (seem, seems) funny.

4. Somebody, either a neighbor or a passerby, (has, have) already notified the police of the accident.

5. Some of the effects of the tornado (is, are) still visible.

6. Happiest at the victory banquet (was, were) the coach.

7. About a third of the people in attendance (think, thinks) he is right.

8. The company of soldiers (was, were) in their assigned positions.
9. The trained dogs in the circus (jump, jumps) through burning hoops.
10. The signatures on the petition (appear, appears) to have been forged.

ANSWERS

1. looks	2. is	3. seem	4. has
5. are	6. was	7. think	8. were
9. jump	10. appear		

5.2 SUBJECT NUMBER IS NOT ALWAYS EASY TO DETERMINE.

To follow the rule that verbs must agree in number with their subjects, it is necessary to determine whether a subject is singular or plural. That is not always easy to do for several reasons.

Some singular nouns look plural but usually take singular verbs.

EXAMPLES

☐ statistics   ☐ physics   ☐ tactics
☐ electronics   ☐ athletics   ☐ politics
☐ news   ☐ measles   ☐ economics

☐ The *news is* good.
☐ *Physics was* his major study in college.

Some nouns, as you learned in Lesson 2.2, are spelled the same in both the singular and the plural form. Among them are *deer*, *sheep*, *species*, *corps*, and *headquarters*.

☐ The firm's headquarters is in Boston.
   (singular)

☐ His sheep was in the pasture.
   (singular — only one sheep)

☐ His sheep were in the pasture.
   (plural — more than one sheep)

Such words as *pant*, *scale*, and *scissor* are most often used in the singular form with plural spelling.

☐ The scale *is* in the next room.
   (one scale)

☐ The scales *are* in the next room.
   (either one or more than one)

☐ His pants *are* torn.
   (one pair)

☐ The scissors (*is*, *are*) broken.
   (either is correct)

The plural of fish is either *fish* or *fishes*, with *fish* most commonly used.

You learned in your study of nouns in Lesson 2.2 that some words from Latin and Greek keep their original spelling in the plural. They look singular but are actually plural.

Singular	*Plural*
criterion	criteria
datum	data
bacterium	bacteria
alga	algae
stimulus	stimuli
alumnus*	alumni

☐   The data were misleading.
☐   The alumni are meeting in the auditorium.

■   **Most generally the word *number* is singular when it is preceded by the article *the* and plural when it is preceded by the article *a*.**

☐   The number *has* grown enormously.
        (singular)
☐   A number of members *were* absent.
        (plural)

■   **A compound subject is plural.**

☐   Tina and Dianne *are* college students.
☐   Tina and Dianne and I *are* related.

Two rules apply to compound subjects connected by such conjunctions as *or*, *nor*, *either ... or*, and *neither ... nor*.

---

*   Alumnus is the masculine singular form; alumni is plural; alumna is singular feminine; alumnae is plural feminine.

1. **If two or more singular subjects are connected by that kind of conjunction, the verb must be singular.**

- ☐ Either Betty or Frank *is* in the garden.
- ☐ Neither Betty nor Frank *knows* we are here.

2. **If one subject is singular and one is plural in a compound subject, the noun or pronoun nearer the verb determines which form of the verb to use.**

- ☐ Neither Jackie nor her sisters *were* in the garden.
- ☐ Neither the sisters nor *Jackie was* in the garden.

Some grammarians insist that when one subject is singular and one is plural in a compound subject, the plural subject should always be second; that is, the plural subject should be nearer the verb.

Correct: ☐ Neither Mary nor her *sisters were* in the garden.
Incorrect: ☐ Neither her sisters nor *Mary was* in the garden.

■ **A compound subject is considered to be singular when it refers to the same person or thing or expresses a single idea.**

- ☐ My *friend and companion* was with me.
  (one person)
- ☐ His *pastor and counselor* is out of town today.
  (one person)

☐ The changing *shape and size* of the object was puzzling.
(one idea)

As explained in Lesson 2.13, the use of articles with nouns makes a difference in the number expressed and therefore the verb that follows.

EXAMPLES

☐ The president and the chief executive officer *were* present.
(two persons — plural subject, plural verb *were*)
☐ The president and chief executive officer *was* present.
(one person — singular subject, singular verb *was*)

☐ A waiter and a busboy *work* long hours.
(two persons — plural subject, plural verb *work*)
☐ A waiter and busboy *works* long hours.
(one person — singular subject, singular verb *works*)

Forms of the verb *be*, which as you know are such words as *is*, *are*, *was*, *were*, can cause errors in agreement when the subject is singular and the predicate nominative is plural.

EXAMPLES

☐ A hindrance *was* the broken steps.
(singular subject, singular verb)

The subject *hindrance* is singular, so the singular verb *was* is correct. The sentence can be reversed in this manner, so that it has a plural subject.

☐ The broken steps *were* a hindrance.

☐ The problem *was* the sick children.
(singular subject, singular verb)
☐ The sick children *were* the problem.
(plural subject, plural verb)

Not only verbs but also other parts of predicates must agree with the subjects.

EXAMPLES

Correct: ☐ All of the men paid *for their own tickets.*
Incorrect: ☐ All the men paid *for their own ticket.*

Correct: ☐ Some of these thoroughbreds have a chance *to become big winners.*
Incorrect: ☐ Some of these thoroughbreds have a chance *to become a big winner.*

FOR PRACTICE

Underline the correct verbs in parentheses in these sentences.

1. The scale in the laboratory (was, were) found to be inaccurate.
2. The criteria for judging the entries (was, were) announced today.
3. Neither the workers on the assembly line nor the foremen in the shop (seem, seems) pleased with the decision.
4. The bookkeeper and cashier (believe, believes) the figure is correct.
5. Both the bookkeeper and the cashier (believe, believes) the figure is correct.
6. The difficulty in traveling (was, were) the bad roads.
7. Neither Senior Perez nor Senora Perez (was, were) at home.
8. Politics (is, are) defined as the art of government.
9. The number of no votes (was, were) dismaying.
10. The taste and texture of the cake (was, were) satisfactory.

Now check your answers.

5.3 PRONOUNS MUST AGREE WITH THEIR ANTECEDENTS.

You have learned that most pronouns have antecedents, and that an antecedent is the noun or pronoun that the pronoun stands for.

EXAMPLE

☐ *John* gave me some money; *he* is my friend.

In that sentence the pronoun is *he* which stands for *John*. Thus *John* is the antecedent of *he*.

■ **To be used correctly, pronouns must agree with their antecedents in person, number, and gender.**

In the sentence above, the noun *John* and the pronoun *he* agree because they are both third person, singular number, and masculine gender. Here are more examples in which the pronouns agree with their antecedents.

EXAMPLES

☐ *Cliff* and *his* brother were at the fair.
☐ *They* were in the pavilion. (Antecedent: Cliff and his brother)
☐ *Cliff* attends the fair every year; *he* enjoys it.

As you have learned, the subject is plural when it contains more than one noun or pronoun connected by *and*, even though the nouns and the pronouns are singular.

☐   *Luis and Manuel* were studying *their* lessons.

The pronoun in that sentence, *their*, is plural to agree with its antecedent, *Luis and Manuel*, which is a compound subject and therefore plural.

■   **The subject is singular when two or more singular nouns or pronouns are connected by *or, either...or*, or *neither...nor*.**

☐   Juan or Vincente will bring *his* guitar.
☐   Either Juan or Vincente will bring *his* guitar.
☐   Neither Juan nor Vincente will bring *his* guitar.

You recall, however, that in a compound sentence if the noun or pronoun next to the verb is plural, the subject (the antecedent) is considered plural.

☐   Vincente or his two brothers will bring *their* guitars.

In the previous lesson on agreement of verbs with their subjects, you learned that the key is determining the subject of the verb. Once you know that, you can tell whether the subject is singular or plural and use the form of the verb that agrees with the subject.

In regard to agreement of pronouns with their antecedents, the key is being able to determine which word is the antecedent. You then use the pronoun that agrees in person, number, and gender with its antecedent. Problems can occur, however, when an antecedent is a collective noun or an indefinite pronoun.

Collective nouns as antecedents of pronouns can be troublesome because, as you learned in the previous lesson, collective nouns can be either singular or plural, depending upon the meaning of the sentence.

Usually a collective noun is singular; but when it refers to the members of the group rather than to the group as one entity, it can be used in the plural.

Singular: □ The Board of Directors gave *its* approval.
Plural: □ The Board of Directors accepted *their* assignments willingly.

■ **Indefinite pronouns, listed in Lesson 2.4, do not refer to specific persons or things and do not require antecedents. Some are always singular, some are always plural in meaning, and some may be either singular or plural.**

■ **Indefinite pronouns that are always singular are** *another, anyone, everyone, one, each, either, neither, anything, something, somebody.*

□ *No one* could drive *his* car in the deep snow.
□ *Each* of the drivers adjusted *his* goggles.

■ **Indefinite pronouns that are always plural are** *both, many, few, several, others.*

□ *Both* students were busy at *their* desks.
□ *Many* of us were in *our* homes at the time.

■ **The indefinite pronouns** *all, most, more, half, none, some,* **and** *any* **as well as** *everyone* **and** *everybody* **may be singular or plural, depending upon their meaning in the sentence.**

EXAMPLES

- ☐ Some were hesitant to state *their* opinions.
- ☐ Some of the merchandise was defective; *it* had been mishandled.
- ☐ Everybody in the village came to the meeting, but *they* didn't remain until it adjourned.
- ☐ Everybody brought *his* car to the meeting.

■ **Such pronouns as *all* and *half* can be used in the singular.**

EXAMPLES

- ☐ Half of the team *was* dressed.
- ☐ All *is* ready for the game.

■ **The indefinite pronoun *none* is a special case. Once it was considered singular, but now it may be either singular or plural, depending on the construction of the sentence. In modern usage, *none* is more often used in the plural than in the singular.**

One aspect of the English language that causes problems is that the language has no singular personal pronoun that is both masculine and feminine. There is the singular masculine pronoun *he*, the singular feminine pronoun *she*, and the singular neuter pronoun *it*; but there is no word that means both *he* and *she*. The result is that a plural pronoun is often used incorrectly when the antecedent is singular.

EXAMPLE

Incorrect: ☐ *Everyone* was studying *their* lessons.
                   (singular subject, plural pronoun)

The subject *Everyone* is singular but the pronoun *their* is plural, which is grammatically incorrect as they do not agree in number. Correctly stated, the sentence should read as follows.

☐ *Everyone* was studying *his* lesson.

The objection here is that the indefinite pronoun *Everyone* may include both boys and girls or men and women. To use both *his and her*, as stated here, is awkward.

☐ Everyone was studying *his and her* lesson.

EXAMPLES

Correct:	☐	All of them were busy at *their* desks.
Correct:	☐	Each student was busy at *his* desk.
Correct:	☐	Nobody did *his* best.
Incorrect:	☐	Nobody did *their* best.

■ **Note that *everyone* and *anyone* are written as solid words; but when they are followed by a prepositional phrase, they should be written as two words.**

EXAMPLES

☐ *Every one* in the room was studying his lesson.
☐ *Any one* of the men would lend his car to Janet.

It should be noted that some of the words listed as indefinite pronouns may also be adjectives, depending on their use.

EXAMPLES

Pronoun:	☐	*Some* of the men went to their homes.
Adjective:	☐	*Some* men went to their homes.

In the first sentence, the word *Some* is a pronoun and is the subject of the verb *went*. In the second sentence, the word *Some* modifies the noun *men*, and *men* is the subject of the verb *went*. In either sentence, however, the plural pronoun *their* is correct. In the first sentence the antecedent of *their* is *Some*; in the second sentence the antecedent is *men*.

■   A common error is agreement occurs in use of the adjectives *this* and *these* with the words *kind* and *sort*. Both must be either singular or plural.

EXAMPLES

Correct:		□	this kind of candy
		□	these kinds of candies
		□	this sort of creature
		□	these sorts of creatures
Incorrect:		□	this kinds
		□	these kind
		□	this sorts
		□	these sort

FOR PRACTICE

Underline the correct word or words in parentheses in each of these sentences.

1. The class is waiting for (its, their) teacher.

2. The class was busy with (its, their) lessons.

3. The First National Bank offers (its, their) customers a bonus dividend on savings accounts.

4. Mary and Louise will take us to the market in (her, their) car.

5. Mary or Louise will bring (her, their) car for us to use.

6. Neither the mother nor her three daughters are bringing (her, their) drawings to exhibit.

7. Both the mother and her three daughters are bringing (her, their) drawings to exhibit.

8. Everyone told us about (his, their) relatives who live in Ireland.

9. The City Council left (its, their) winter coats in the vestibule.

10. None would tell us (his name, their names).

11. A person must take (his, his or her) bad luck with the good.

12. (Everyone, Every one) voted for the resolution.

13. (Everyone, Every one) in the room voted in favor of the resolution.

14. She was willing to help every needy person who came to the center that morning by giving (him, them) a box of groceries.

15. Everyone must sign the petition if (he has, they have) not already done so.

ANSWERS

1. its	2. their	3. its	4. their
5. her	6. their	7. their	8. his
9. their	10. their names	11. his	12. Everyone
13. Every one	14. him	15. he has	

5.4 *WHO* AND *WHOM* ARE TROUBLESOME PRONOUNS.

Knowing when to use *who* and when to use *whom* can be puzzling. One complication is that they can function in two ways, as interrogative pronouns and as relative pronouns.

The interrogative pronouns, used for asking questions, are *which, whichever, what, whatever, that, who, whoever, whom, whomever,* and *whose.* Among them, the pronouns *which, whichever, what, whatever, whose,* and *that* never change form, so they present no problems.

EXAMPLES

☐ *What* does he want?
☐ *Which* way will he go?

The relative pronouns *who* and *whoever* do change form, depending on their use in sentences. You recall that *who* is nominative case, *whom* is objective case, and *whose* is possessive case.

Using the possessive *whose* presents little difficulty, so long as you don't confuse *whose* and *who's*. Those two are entirely different; *whose* is a pronoun (in some instances it may be used as an adjective), and *who's* is a contraction meaning *who is*.

EXAMPLES

□   *Who's* on first base?
    (who is)
□   *Whose* book is this?
    (possessive pronoun)

REVIEW OF THE CASE OF *WHO* AND *WHOM*.

EXAMPLES

□   *Who* will bring me some coffee?
    (nominative case, subject of the verb *will bring*)
□   *Who* is it?   ° It is *who*?
    (nominative case, subject of the verb *is* in the first sentence and predicate nominative in the second sentence)
□   Darryl said I was *who*?
    (nominative case, predicate nominative after the verb *was*)
□   Is that not the man *whom* you saw?
    (objective case, object of the verb *saw*)
□   I gave *whom* the coffee?
    (objective case, indirect object of the verb *gave*)
□   To *whom* shall I give the coffee?
    (objective case, object of the preposition *To*)
□   Do we know *whom* to ask to bring the coffee?
    (objective case, subject of the infinitive *to ask*)
□   I was asked to give *whom* the coffee?
    (objective case, object of the infinitive t*o give*)

□   I was thought to be *who*?
(nominative case, object of the infinitive *to be* which has no
subject)
□   He thought John to be *whom*?
(objective case, object of the infinitive *to be* which has a
subject)

The pronouns *who* and *whom* are also troublesome because each
is both singular and plural. The only way to tell whether *who* or *whom*
is singular or plural is to determine its antecedent. If the antecedent is
singular, the pronoun is singular; and if the antecedent is plural, the
pronoun is plural. That is necessary in order to have a verb agree with
its subject.

EXAMPLE

□   She is one of those women *who* believe in astrology.

In that sentence, the antecedent of the pronoun *who* is *women*, not
she or *one*. As women is plural, the pronoun *who* is therefore plural, so
the verb must be *believe*, not *believes*, in order to agree.

■   **If the expression is *one of those*, you know that the pronoun
who that follows is plural because its antecedent is *those*, which is
plural. If, on the other hand, the expression is *the kind of man who*,
you know that the pronoun *who* is singular because its antecedent
man is singular.**

Being able to determine whether *who* is singular or plural is
important in regard to agreement of subject and verb.

EXAMPLE

Singular: □   She is the kind of woman *who talks* rapidly.
Plural: □   She is one of those women *who talk* rapidly.

Perhaps that needs further explanation because a prepositional phrase between the subject and the verb can be puzzling. The rule is that the verb must always agree with its subject in number and person.

EXAMPLES

- One *of those truck drivers* was present.
- Wilson is one *of those truck drivers*.
- Wilson is one *of those truck drivers* who were present.
- Wilson is one *of those truck drivers* who work long hours.
- Wilson is a *truck driver* who works long hours.

The first two of those examples are simple sentences. The subject in the first is *One*, the verb is *was*. In the second sentence the subject is *Wilson* and the verb is *is*. Both subjects and verbs are singular in number, and the prepositional phrase in each modifies *one*.

The third and fourth sentences are complex. The subject in each independent clause is *Wilson* and the verb is *is*, both of which are singular. In the third sentence, the antecedent of the pronoun *who* in the dependent clause is *drivers*, so *who* is plural and the verb must be *were* to agree in number. The same is true in the fourth sentence where the antecedent of the pronoun *who* is *drivers* and the verb *work* is plural to agree with the plural pronoun. In the last sentence the antecedent of *who* is *a truck driver*, which is singular.

■ **The interrogative pronoun *who* is widely used in informal speech when *whom* is grammatically correct.**

EXAMPLES

Informal: □ *Who* shall we invite?
Formal: □ *Whom* shall we invite?

Informal: □ *Who* do you want to win?
Formal: □ *Whom* do you want to win?

Sometimes substituting a personal pronoun for *who* or *whom* to see if it sounds right will help indicate the correct form.

EXAMPLES

☐ Milton asked (who, whom) was going with us.
Now state it this way: Is *he* or *him* going with us? As *he* (nominative case) sounds right and is correct, *who* is the correct form.

☐ (Who, Whom) do you want to win?
Restated: Do you want *they* or *them* to win? As *them* (objective case) sounds right and is correct, *whom* is the correct form.

☐ The party was given for (who, whom)?
Restated: The party was given for *he or him*? As *him* (objective case) sounds right and is correct, *whom* is the correct form.

FOR PRACTICE

Underline the correct pronoun in each of these sentences.

1. (Whose, Who's) driving your car?
2. (Who, Whom) was it sent to?
3. They thought I was (who, whom)?
4. The police asked (whoever, whomever) happened to have seen the accident to call the station.
5. He is the man (who, whom) coaches rate as the best forward in local basketball circles.
6. He wanted to give thanks to (whoever, whomever) returned the money.
7. The director of the state fair (who, whom) people say is an able administrator was formerly vice president of a brokerage firm.
8. She is the woman (who, whom) we met in Montreal.
9. She is the woman (who, whom) told us about Montreal.

10. You asked (who, whom) to bring us the books?

11. He believed that strange girl to be (who, whom)?

12. She was believed to be (who, whom)?

13. He handed (who, whom) the check?

14. Bruce said she was (who, whom)?

15. You saw (who, whom) at the market?

ANSWERS

1. Who's (who is)
2. Whom (object of the preposition — it was sent *to whom?*)
3. who (predicate nominative)
4. whoever (subject of the verb *happened*)
5. whom (object of the verb — coaches rate whom)
6. whoever (subject of the verb returned — whoever returned)
7. who (subject of the verb *is* — who is)
8. whom (object of the verb *met* — we met whom)
9. who (subject of the verb *told* — who told us)
10. whom (subject of the infinitive *to bring*)
11. whom (object of the infinitive *to be*)
12. who (object of the infinitive *to be* which has no subject)
13. whom (indirect object of the verb *handed*)
14. who (predicate nominative)
15. whom (object of the verb *saw*)

5.5 *THIS* AND *THAT* ARE CALLED DEMONSTRATIVE PRONOUNS.

■ The four demonstrative pronouns, *this, that, these,* and *those,* are used to point out specific persons and things. They also have other uses.

This is singular; *these* is the plural form. *That* is singular; *those* is the plural form. Those four words are called *demonstrative pronouns*.

They can function as the subjects of sentences, as shown here.

EXAMPLES

- □ *This* is a red flower.
- □ *These* are beautiful flowers.
- □ *That* is a hybrid flower.
- □ *Those* are perennial flowers.

They can also function as adjectives, as illustrated here, and thus may be called *demonstrative adjectives*.

EXAMPLES

- □ *This* flower is red.
- □ *These* flowers are beautiful.
- □ *That* flower is a hybrid.
- □ *Those* flowers are perennials.

The word *that* is rather special in that it can be used in these ways:

1. As a *demonstrative pronoun*, which indicates a specific person, place, or thing.

EXAMPLE

- □ *That* is the best cake you have ever baked.

2. As a *demonstrative adjective,* which modifies a specific person, place, or thing.

EXAMPLES

- □ *That* man is my uncle.
- □ Who was *that* woman in the garden?

3. As an *interrogative pronoun*, which introduces a question.

EXAMPLE

- □ *That* is what you want me to do?

4. As an *adverb*, modifying a predicate adjective.

EXAMPLES

- □ The building was *that* tall.
- □ I learned to read when I was *that* young.

5. As a *subordinating conjunction*, which connects dependent clauses to independent clauses to form complex sentences.

EXAMPLE

- □ Pamela wished *that* the rains would come soon.

6. As a *relative pronoun*, which introduces a dependent clause in a complex sentence.

EXAMPLES

- □ This is the house *that* Jack built.
- □ Nexus is the horse *that* won the race.

The difference in the use of *that* as a relative pronoun and as a subordinating conjunction can be puzzling. Remember that a relative pronoun introduces an adjective clause and a subordinating conjunction introduces an adverb clause.

In the sentence, This is the house that Jack built, the dependent clause, *that Jack built,* modifies the noun *house* and thus is an adjective clause. In the next sentence, Nexus is the horse that won the race, the dependent clause, *that won the race*, modifies the noun *horse* and thus is an adjective clause.

In the sentence, Pamela wished that the rains would come soon, the dependent clause, *that the rains would come soon*, modifies the verb *wished* by telling what she wished and thus is an adverb clause.

Another special use of *that* is that it is frequently an unspoken part of a complex sentence.

EXAMPLE

    ☐ I think I am ready to go now.

Although that sentence may appear to be compound, formed by two independent clauses, it is in fact complex. The independent clause is *I think* and the dependent clause is *(that) I am ready to go now.* The subordinating conjunction *that* is not stated but is understood. That is common in the English language in both speech and writing.

EXAMPLES

    ☐ We wish (that) he would come home.
    ☐ I am sure (that) I was welcome.

FOR PRACTICE

Write in the blank opposite each sentence whether the word *that* is used as a demonstrative adjective, a demonstrative pronoun, a relative pronoun, a subordinating conjunction, or an adverb.

1. That is an interesting book. _____

2. The string was about that long. _____

3. That computer is a gift from my uncle. _____

4. He said that he was ready to go. _____

5. He has an oil painting that is priceless. _____

6. That was an enjoyable occasion. _____

7. That girl saw the accident happen. _____

8. Mary hoped that the rain would stop soon. _____

9. It was his advice that helped me most. _____

10. That is what you asked me? _____

ANSWERS

1. Demonstrative Pronoun   2. Adverb
3. Demonstrative Adjective   4. Subordinating Conjunction
5. Relative Pronoun   6. Demonstrative Pronoun
7. Demonstrative Adjective   8. Subordinating Conjunction
9. Relative Pronoun   10. Interrogative Pronoun

5.6 THE PRONOUN TO USE DEPENDS UPON THE MEANING.

Choosing the correct case of pronouns in implied comparison that uses the words *as* and *then* can be puzzling. In these examples, should the pronoun in parenthesis be *I* (nominative case) or *me* (objective case)? Can you tell why you selected the nominative or the objective case?

EXAMPLES

- He is *as* tall *as* (I, me).
- He is taller *than* (I, me).

The pronoun *I* (nominative case) should be used in each sentence because there is an implied or unfinished comparison. The real meaning is this.

- He is as tall as *I am tall.*
- He is taller than *I am tall.*

But the nominative case is not always correct; whether you use nominative or objective depends on what you mean. These two sentences will illustrate.

EXAMPLES

- He gave Henry as much candy as *me*.
- He gave Henry as much candy as *I*.

The first sentence means, He gave Henry as much candy *as he gave me*. The second sentence means, He gave Henry as much candy *as I gave Henry*. In the first sentence *me* (objective case) is the indirect object of the verb *gave*, or you may wish to think of *me* in that sentence as the object of the preposition *to* understood (*as he gave to me*). In the second sentence *I* is the subject of the verb *gave*.

EXAMPLES

- My sister visits our parents more than me.
- My sister visits our parents more than I.

The first sentence means, My sister visits our parents more than she visits me. The second sentence means, My sister visits our parents more than I visit them.

In some implied comparisons, however, the pronoun *me* cannot correctly be used.

- ☐ Louis is older than I (not me).
  With implied words: Louis is older than I (am old).

- ☐ Louis works harder than I (not me).
  With implied word: Louis works harder than I (work).

- ☐ Louis plays tennis better than I (not me).
  With implied words: Louis plays tennis better than I (play tennis).

In this kind of implied comparison, the meaning determines which pronoun to use.

- ☐ He dislikes Dexter as much as me.
- ☐ He dislikes Dexter as much as I.

When the implied words are filled in, the correct usage becomes clear.

- ☐ He dislikes Dexter as much as (he dislikes) me.
- ☐ He dislikes Dexter as much as I (dislike Dexter).

FOR PRACTICE

Underline the correct pronoun in parenthesis in each of these five sentences; then complete the sentence to indicate why you have used that particular pronoun.

EXAMPLES

☐ Francisco works harder than (I, me).
Answer: Francisco works harder than (*I*, me) *work*.

☐ Louise visits our grandmother oftener than (I, me).
Answer: Louise visits our grandmother oftener than (*I*, me) *visit our grandmother*.
or   Louise visits our grandmother oftener than (I, *me*) *she visits me*.

1. The teacher helps Ann more than (I, me).   _____
2. Louis is not as active as (she, her).   _____
3. My uncle treats my brother better than (I, me). _____
4. My sister attended school more than (I, me).   _____
5. My brother is more diplomatic than (I, me).   _____

ANSWERS

1. The teacher helps Ann more than I. *I help Ann.*
or The teacher helps Ann more than me. *She helps me.*
2. Louis is not as active as she. *She is active.*
3. My uncle treats my brother better than I. *I treat my brother.*
or My uncle treats my brother better than me. *He treats me.*
4. My sister attended school more than I. *I attended school.*
5. My brother is more diplomatic than I. *I am diplomatic.*

REVIEW OF AGREEMENT

If you feel you are not yet quite clear on the use of *who* and *whom*, here is further review for you.

Which is correct, *Who is who*? or *Who is whom*?

Who is who is correct because the second *who* is a predicate nominative. Here are more sentences containing *who* and *whom*.

☐   (Who, Whom) did you say is our guide?

The pronoun *Who* is correct because it is the subject of the verb, Who is our guide? Actually, *Who* is used as an interrogative pronoun in that sentence, although that makes no difference in its form.

☐   Do you know (who, whom) they are?

Again, *who* is correct because it is a predicate nominative. Read the sentence this way: they are who.

☐   (Who, Whom) did you say the Council chose?

Here the correct pronoun is *Whom* as it is the object of the verb *chose.* The Council chose whom?

☐   He told (who, whom) the story?

In that sentence, the correct pronoun is *whom* because it is the indirect object of the verb *told.*

☐   You want me to help (who, whom)?

The correct pronoun is *whom* as it is the object of infinitive *to help*.

☐   You wanted (who, whom) to call me?

Here the correct pronoun is *whom* because it is the subject of the infinitive *to call.*

☐   You sent the letter to (who, whom)?

The correct pronoun is *whom* as it is the object of the preposition *to.*

TEST ON AGREEMENT

Now test yourself by underlining the correct word in parenthesis in each of these sentences.

1. (Who, Whom), I wondered, will be elected?
2. You wanted (who, whom) to be elected?
3. (Who, Whom) did he appoint?
4. Robert gave (who, whom) the racquet?
5. That is the man (who, whom) the police said is dangerous?
6. (Who, Whom) were you talking about?
7. He is a candidate (who, whom) I believe will make a good councilman.
8. I will give a prize to (whoever, whomever) gives the correct answer.
9. I can see (whoever, whomever) comes through the door.
10. (Who, Whom) shall we invite to the party?

Then check your answers to see how well you have done.

Next, check yourself on your knowledge of the agreement of pronouns with their antecedents, by underlining the correct word in parentheses in these sentences.

11. Every member of the club should do (his, their) part.
12. Either James or Paul will drive (his, their) car.
13. A person can improve (his, their) knowledge by using the library.
14. Neither Mary nor Janice was aware of (her, their) danger.
15. Someone thought (he, they) could do it better.
16. Put everything in (its, their) place.
17. Michael and James have completed (his, their) work.
18. Each woman has a room for (herself, themselves).

19. Anyone could lose (his, their) way in that dense forest.

20. Either the boy or the girls will make (herself, themselves) known when you arrive.

21. Few were satisfied with (his, their) pay.

22. Neither the coach nor the players said they knew anything about that rule when (he, they) talked to the reporter.

23. Everybody present expressed (his, their) opinion.

24. Some did not want to express (his, their) opinions.

25. Was it Jorge or Andrew who lost (his, their) money?

Underline the verb in each sentence that agrees with its subject.

26. In the car (is, are) three small children.

27. He (doesn't, don't) work every day.

28. The men in the field (work, works) till 5 o'clock.

29. A third of the men (go, goes) home at sundown.

30. The teacher and discussion leader (was, were) pointing to a chart.

31. The teacher and the discussion leader (was, were) pointing to a chart.

32. Twenty dollars (is, are) enough to pay for it.

33. A number of the birds (was, were) wading near the shore.

34. The number of birds (was, were) increasing very day.

35. Neither Martha nor John (is, are) willing to go.

36. The trees on the hillside (grow, grows) tall.

37. Ten years (is, are) called a decade.

38. The question of electing a president, as well as locating a new office for the firm, (need, needs) serious study.

39. The difficulty (was, were) too many books to read.

40. Busiest of all (was, were) the women in the kitchen.

41. That city, which operates several expensive governmental departments, (levy, levies) a high tax on real property.

42. The data (was, were) discussed in an open meeting.

43. Economics (is, are) concerned with the production, distribution, and consumption of goods and services.

44. The class (has, have) turned in their term papers.

45. William, together with the Boy Scouts, (was, were) busy studying for the next test.

Finally a mixture with which to test yourself by underlining the correct word in parentheses in these sentences.

46. From many experiments (come, comes) a useful scientific fact.

47. The data in this book (is, are) correct.

48. The dog wagged (its, it's) tail.

49. He is one of those jovial spirits who (make, makes) everyone happy.

50. (Sit, Set) on that chair, please.

51. Between you and (I, me), I don't believe his story.

52. Do you mind (me, my) making a suggestion?

53. This automobile is (theirs, their's, theirs').

54. Certainly I wouldn't want to be (he, him).

55. It was they who (was, were) seen fishing.

56. No one except legislators (was, were) sent a notice of the meeting.

57. I believe this book is (yours, your's).

58. (Who, Whom) did you say is going?

59. Behind John and (I, me) walked the headmaster.

60. We want to arrange the data so (it, they) can be reviewed annually.

61. My sister together with several neighbors (is, are) going to the fair.

62. They are the kind who (like, likes) to travel on ocean liners.

63. The other woman or Mary alone (has, have) responsibility in this matter.

64. The length of road races about the country (range, ranges) from a mile to many miles.

65. (You, Your) giving money to that beggar surprised me.

66. A statement of procedures and practices (was, were) adopted by the Student Council.

67. None of the officers (was, were) available for comment.

68. Any one of the horses (appear, appears) able to win the race.

69. A number of persons (has, have) asked about that.

70. If I were (he, him), I would go.

Now check your answers to see how well you have done.

ANSWERS

1.	Who	2.	whom	3.	Whom	4.	whom
5.	who	6.	Whom	7.	who	8.	whoever
9.	whoever	10.	Whom	11.	his	12.	his
13.	his	14.	her	15.	he	16.	its
17.	their	18.	herself	19.	his	20.	themselves
21.	their	22.	they	23.	his	24.	their
25.	his	26.	are	27.	doesn't	28.	work
29.	go	30.	was	31.	were	32.	is
33.	were	34.	was	35.	is	36.	grow
37.	is	38.	needs	39.	was	40.	were
41.	levies	42.	were	43.	is	44.	have
45.	was	46.	comes	47.	are	48.	its
49.	make	50.	Sit	51.	me	52.	my
53.	theirs	54.	he	55.	were	56.	was
57.	yours	58.	Who	59.	me	60.	they
61.	is	62.	like	63.	has	64.	ranges
65.	Your	66.	was	67.	were	68.	appears
69.	have	70.	he				

6

BUILDING BETTER SENTENCES

The first fifty-five lessons in this book explain
the basic rules and principles of English grammar. They are devoted to syntax, to the way
words, phrases, and clauses are put together to
form sentences. But grammar's main purpose
is to enhance communication by adding clarity
and beauty to the language.

In the concluding five lessons the emphasis
is not so much on grammar as it is on ways to
assure greater clarity and harmony in writing.
Among those ways are the use of parallel structure, the inclusion of only related ideas in sentences, avoidance of shifts in voice and tense,
alertness for unintended implications, not over-
loading sentences with ideas, understanding
emphasis and subordination, and the use of
figurative language.

6.1 PARALLEL SENTENCES CONTAIN PARALLEL IDEAS.

Ideas that are parallel in thought should be parallel in structure. You can easily see that the following sentence is faulty in that respect.

EXAMPLE

☐ He likes batting and to play first base.

The word *batting* is a gerund and the words *to play* an infinitive. To be parallel, the sentence should read as follows.

☐ He likes *batting* and *playing* first base.
or ☐ He likes *to bat* and *to play* first base.

Lack of parallel structure can occur more readily in sentences that are longer.

EXAMPLE

☐ Among the things that make my employment in this company attractive are, first, making friends; second, because there is opportunity for advancement; and third, the retirement plan.

That sentence may be rewritten in this manner so that is has parallel structure.

☐ Among the things that make my employment in this company attractive are, first, *the friends* I make; second, *the opportunity* I have for advancement; and third, *the retirement plan* I participate in.

or ☐ Among the things that make my employment in this company attractive are *making* friends, *having* opportunity for advancement, and *participating* in the retirement plan.

In both of those examples a similar grammatical construction is used to give the sentences parallel structure, which makes them easier to understand.

■   **A well-constructed sentence does not contain a shift in voice.**

In Lesson 2.8 you learned that verbs have voice and may be either active voice or passive voice.

EXAMPLES

Active voice: □   Tina wore a red dress.
Passive voice: □   A red dress was worn by Tina.

The following examples illustrate shifts in voice within single sentences and the preferable parallel structures.

EXAMPLES

Shift from active to passive voice:

□   Mr. and Mrs. Anderson owed the firm $40, but it *was not paid* by them.

Parallel Structure:

□   Mr. and Mrs. Anderson owed the firm $40, but they *did not pay* it.

Shift from active to passive voice:

□   His grandmother *gave* him a gift of money, and a few days later he *was given* a bicycle.

Parallel Structure:

□   His grandmother *gave* him a gift of money, and a few days later she *gave* him a bicycle.

■ **The careful writer also avoids shifts in tense and mood.**

Shift in tense:

□ The story is about a boy and a girl who *fall* in love, *married*, and *lived* happily ever after.

In that sentence the verb *fall* is present tense while the verbs *married* and *lived* are past tense. All should be in the same tense, either past or present. It may read as follows:

□ The story was about a boy and a girl who *fell* in love, *married*, and *lived* happily ever after.

or □ The story is about a boy and a girl who *fall* in love, *marry*, and *live* happily ever after.

Shift in mood:

□ If I *were* wealthy enough and my brother *was* healthy enough, we would go on an ocean cruise.

The sentence would be improved if *was* were changed to *were* so the two verbs would be in agreement. It would then read as follows:

□ If I *were* wealthy enough and my brother *were* healthy enough, we would go on an ocean cruise.

■ **Generally, the careful writer avoids splitting infinitives. A split infinitive is one that has one or more words dividing the infinitive; that is, between the *to* and the *verb*.**

□ He wanted *to quickly finish* his work.
(to finish)

□ He decided *to before returning home eat* dinner in the cafe. (to eat)

Those sentences would be improved if rewritten in this manner.

□ He wanted *to finish* his work quickly.
□ He decided *to eat* dinner in the cafe before returning home.

In some cases, splitting an infinitive can be avoided by revising the sentence. In some sentences, however, it is better to split an infinitive in order to avoid an awkward or ambiguous construction.

EXAMPLE

□ The Democrats support a move *to fully fund* last year's bill.

That is preferable to *fully to fund* or t*o fund fully*. It is important to be aware of split infinitives and to use the construction that is clearest and sounds best.

FOR PRACTICE

Underline the parallel elements in these sentences.

EXAMPLE

□ Owning a station wagon is a convenience not only *for me* but also *for my family*.

1. Do you advise me to invest in stocks, to start a savings account, or to buy government bonds?
2. I think playing bridge calls for more skill than playing gin rummy.
3. He was obeyed by his soldiers, feared by his servants, and hated by his enemies.

Now test yourself by rewriting these sentences to improve them.

Parallel structure

4. Marie likes working in an office more than to cook meals at home.

5. We should do these things to improve living conditions, increasing the value of our property, and for keeping our community spirit strong.

Shift in voice

6. Joanne washed the supper dishes and then some sewing was done by her.

7. The committee discussed the projects for more than an hour, but not many points were agreed upon.

Shift in tense

8. After we ate supper, he goes to the bowling lanes.

9. First he shouted his objection to the proposal and then he stalks out of the room.

Shift in mood

10. If he were here and I was with him, we would decide immediately what to do.

11. Go to college first and then you should get a job.

Split infinitive

12. We need volunteers to lovingly devote their time as their gift in this Christmas Season.

13. He asked us to immediately notify the office of the change.

ANSWERS

1. to invest in stocks, to start a savings account, to buy government bonds

2. playing bridge, playing gin rummy
3. obeyed by his soldiers, feared by his servants, hated by his enemies
4. Marie likes working in an office more than cooking meals at home.
5. We should do these things to improve living conditions, to increase the value of our property, and to keep our community spirit strong.
6. Joanne washed the supper dishes and then did some sewing.
7. The committee discussed the project for more than an hour, but it did not agree on many points.
8. After we ate supper, he went to the bowling lanes. (or) After we eat supper, he goes to the bowling lanes.
9. First he shouted his objection to the proposal, and then he stalked out of the room.
10. If he were here and I were with him (or) If he was here and I was with him, we would decide immediately what to do.
11. Go to college first and then get a job. (or) You should go to college first and then you should get a job.
12. We need volunteers to devote their time lovingly as their gift...
13. He asked us to notify the office immediately of the change.

6.2 IDEAS IN A SENTENCE SHOULD BE RELATED.

A sentence should contain only related ideas. Here are examples of sentences that contain unrelated ideas.

EXAMPLES

☐ Winter arrived late that year, and my sister played familiar tunes on the piano.

☐ Dr. Johnson is a specialist in neurosurgery and has a basset hound which he calls Ha-Ha.

☐   The centennial of the Statute of Liberty was celebrated in 1986, and our son graduated from college.

Sentences of that kind can be rewritten to show relationship between the ideas they contain.

EXAMPLES

☐   Winter arrived late that year; and when we were housebound in bad weather, my sister played familiar tunes on the piano.

☐   Dr. Johnson, a specialist in neurosurgery, relaxes from his work by taking walks with his basset hound, which he calls Ha-Ha.

☐   Two events in 1986 stand out in our memory. One was the celebration of the Statue of Liberty centennial; the other was our son's graduation from college.

When you read what you have written, check to see that ideas in sentences, and indeed in paragraphs, are related. When they are not, you need to do some rewriting.

■   **The careful writer guards against unintended implications in his writing. This is necessary because many English sentences have or can have two meanings, one that is stated and one that is implied.**

For example, the sentence, "The sun is shining," clearly means just that. However, depending upon the occasion in which it is used, it could also have an implied meaning. It could imply that "The storm has ended," or "The sun is shining even though the rain is still falling," or "Now is the time to take some outdoor photographs," or a dozen other things.

Unintended implications are deceptively easy to write.

EXAMPLES

- [ ] The coach said that better protective headgear for football players costs more than the school can afford.
  Implication: School administrators are willing to risk injury to players.

- [ ] The Human Relations Center was created on the campus last February when the need to assist disadvantaged youth was finally recognized.
  Implication: In all the years past university officials had failed to recognize the needs of disadvantaged youth.

- [ ] Her agent, Albert Fredan, failed to check the rules and entered her in the contest despite her age.
  Implication: The agent was either lazy or careless.

Extreme brevity may lead to unintended implications.

EXAMPLES

- [ ] The November 30 robbery of the Kent Ellis Hotel...
  Implication: There have been other robberies at that hotel.
  That implication could be avoided by writing it this way:
- [ ] The robbery of the Kent Ellis Hotel on November 30...

- [ ] A Catholic, he was elected mayor.
  Implication: He was elected mayor because he was a Catholic.

Incomplete identification can obscure clarity.

EXAMPLES

- [ ] James Furman will be playing with the Centerville Hornets next season. On Monday the left-handed pitcher signed a three-year contract with that team.

It is not quite clear that the left-handed pitcher mentioned in the second sentence is James Furman, although it may be. Doubt would be removed if it were written this way:

☐ James Furman will be playing with the Centerville Hornets next season. A left-handed pitcher, he signed a three-year contract with that team on Monday.

FOR PRACTICE

1. This sentence contains unrelated ideas. Restate it, subordinating one of the ideas.
☐ Harry Anderson is my friend, and he has a large herd of Holstein cattle.

2. What is the implication of this sentence?
☐ Born in Haiti, he was denied membership in the Club.

3. What is implied in this excerpt of a news story about a fire?
☐ The Fire Chief said that the fire alarm apparently was not working. Records show that the alarm had been checked by a city inspector only two weeks ago.

4. Clarity: Which team is the Trojans?
☐ Troy won 78-76 in overtime Thursday night in a home game with Centerville. The Trojans set a record by making 75 per cent of their field goal attempts.

5. Clarity: Which player is the Austrian?
☐ Thomas Muster rallied from a 3-0 deficit in the final set to defeat Jimmy Arias 3-6, 6-2, and 7-5 and win the Hardcourt Tennis Championship in Adelaide yesterday. The Austrian had largely recovered from an injury received in an automobile accident last April.

ANSWERS

1. Harry Anderson, a friend of mine, has a large herd of Holstein cattle.
2. He was denied membership because he was a native Haitian.
3. The records may have been falsified or the inspection was faulty.
4. Adding one word in the second sentence would make clear that the Trojans were the Troy team: The *winning* Trojans or The *Troy* Trojans...
5. Also, the second sentence could read: Muster, an Austrian, had ...
   Sentences should be so clear that the reader does not have to guess.

6.3 FOR CLARITY, VERBS SHOULD BE CLOSE TO THEIR SUBJECTS.

The reader can become confused when a verb is separated from its subject by a number of words.

EXAMPLE

☐ *The mob*, urged on by bystanders and energetic leaders and apparently facing little opposition from the police a block away, *surged* toward the doorway.

The subject is *the mob* and the verb is *surged*, but they are separated by 18 words. The sentence would be improved it it read:

☐ *The mob surged* toward the doorway, urged on by bystanders and energetic leaders and apparently facing little opposition from the police a block away.

The reader can also become confused in attempting to read a sentence that is overloaded with ideas.

□   A tight supply situation may develop in the nation's major farm products with the possible exception of cotton before this summer's harvest gets under way, because surplus stocks have been virtually exhausted through heavy shipments abroad, which is the first time that has happened in more than ten years.

That would be easier to read if it were broken into two or three sentences.

□   A tight supply situation may develop in the nation's major farm products with the possible exception of cotton before this summer's harvest gets under way. The reason is that surplus stocks have been virtually exhausted through heavy shipments abroad. This is the first time that has happened in more than ten years.

Here is another example of an overloaded sentence.

□   Faculty members involved in a project at both schools this spring, plus some pupils and parents, were given the opportunity to assess progress in a survey coordinated by Jacob Schaum, former counselor now serving in the Personnel Administration Division, and conducted under the supervision of Assistant Superintendent David Studer.

That sentence would be clearer and more easily understood if it were broken into three sentences.

☐ Faculty members involved in the project at both schools this spring, plus some pupils and parents, were given the opportunity to assess progress. That was done through a survey coordinated by Jacob Schaum, former counselor now serving in the Personnel Administration Division. The survey was conducted under the supervision of David Studer, assistant superintendent.

The opposite of overloaded sentences is too much brevity. Here is a sentence, for example, that attempts to say that more out-of-state students at Kent State University in Ohio come from Pennsylvania than any other state; but it fails to do so because it is so brief.

EXAMPLE

☐ Pennsylvania sends the most non-residents to Kent State University.

Although unnecessary words should be omitted, it is well to remember that words are necessary to express a thought, to explain a condition, and to describe an object or situation or event. A sufficient number of words should be used to make the meaning clear to the reader.

FOR PRACTICE

Rewrite each of these sentences to bring the subject and the verb closer. To do so, you will need to break each long sentence into two sentences.

1. The old farm house, neglected for years, half hidden by overgrown shrubbery and covered with vines, the white paint applied years ago now peeling and the red brick chimney askew, stood at the end of a tree-lined lane about a tenth of a mile from the highway.

2. Mrs. Gonzales, pronounced dead at the scene of the fire at 1127 Second Avenue apparently of smoke inhalation but with burns on portions of her body, had been trying to make her way to the sliding glass door leading to the balcony when she was overcome.

3. Arthur Monet, well-known local businessman who has twice been a candidate for city councilman and was a strong supporter of Mayor Johnson in a recent dispute over relocation of a juvenile correction facility, announced yesterday that he has sold his business and is moving to Atlanta.

4. The historic Raxton Mill, an old frame building on the Durham River a mile east of Carlton near the site of a fierce battle in the French and Indian Wars and a gathering place for farmers bringing grain for milling in the 18th century, was destroyed by fire last night.

5. Alexander Andressa, local television show host who won recognition in Rochester for his success in building a large audience for an innovative interview program before coming to this city as an announcer, is leaving the broadcast industry to accept a teaching position at Maynard College.

ANSWERS

1. The old farm house stood at the end of a tree-lined lane about a tenth of a mile from the highway. Neglected for years, it was half hidden by overgrown shrubbery and covered with vines, the white paint applied years ago now peeling and the red brick chimney askew.

2. Mrs. Gonzales was pronounced dead at the scene of the fire at 1127 Second Avenue, apparently of smoke inhalation but with burns on portions of her body. It is believed that she had been trying to make her way to the sliding glass door leading to the balcony when she was overcome with smoke.

3. Arthur Monet, well-known businessman, announced yesterday that he had sold his business and is moving to Atlanta. He has twice been a candidate for the city council and was a strong supporter of Mayor Johnson in a recent dispute over relocation of a juvenile correction facility.

4. The historic Raxton Mill was destroyed by fire last night. It was an old frame building on the Durham River a mile east of Carlton near the site of a fierce battle in the French and Indian wars and a gathering place in the 18th century for farmers bringing grain for milling .

5. Alexander Andressa, local television show host, is leaving the broadcast industry to accept a teaching position at Maynard College. He won recognition in Rochester for his success in building a large audience for an innovative interview program before coming to this city as an announcer.

6.4 EMPHASIS AND SUBORDINATION AFFECT THE MEANING.

Everyone uses emphasis and subordination when he writes, whether he realizes it or not. Emphasis and subordination can be effected in several ways:

■ **A word or words are emphasized when they are placed first in a sentence; they are subordinated when they are placed last or inside the sentence.**

EXAMPLES

☐ Six airplanes and four helicopters searched thousands of square miles of the Amazon, looking for the lost Brazilian jetliner.

☐ Thousands of square miles of the Amazon were searched by six airplanes and four helicopters, looking for the lost Brazilian jetliner.

The first sentence emphasizes the number of search craft being used by giving the number of them at the beginning of the sentence. The second sentence emphasizes the area being searched by naming that first.

■ **The meaning can be affected by changing the emphasis.**

EXAMPLES

☐ Jason played golf yesterday.

That sentence is merely a statement of fact; but suppose it is written, or spoken, with the word *Yesterday* first.

☐ Yesterday Jason played golf.

In that sentence the emphasis is given to the word *Yesterday* which conveys a subtle implication that today he is playing some other game, or yesterday Jason was well but today he is ill, or even dead.

■ **Ideas are emphasized when they are placed in independent clauses; they are subordinated when they are placed in dependent clauses.**

EXAMPLE

☐ Dr. James B. Bruner, superintendent of schools, was guest speaker at the annual banquet of the Chamber of Commerce last night.

That sentence emphasizes that Dr. Bruner was the speaker, that he spoke. The next example provides a different emphasis.

EXAMPLE

☐ Personnel improvement and adequate financing are now the major problems facing local schools, Dr. J. B. Bruner, superintendent, said last night. Speaking at the annual banquet of the Chamber of Commerce, the superintendent outlined school problems as he has found them since his arrival here three months ago.

When stated that way, emphasis is given to what Dr. Bruner said, not to the fact that he spoke.

■ **Among other means of giving emphasis are placing a word or words at the end of the sentence, although that is not as emphatic as placing them at the beginning, using active voice rather than passive voice, and repeating important words and phrases.**

Sentences are usually more forceful and less wordy when they are written in active voice. That does not mean, however, that passive voice should never be used. For instance, a different emphasis may require the use of passive voice. That can be illustrated with these two "news briefs."

EXAMPLES

Active voice: ☐ Highland Park — Forest Rangers shot and killed a bear that menaced square dancers in a recreation hall here last night.

Passive voice: ☐ Highland Park — A bear was shot and killed by Forest Rangers here last night when it menaced square dancers in a recreation hall.

In the first, *Forest Rangers* is emphasized by being placed first in the sentence; in the second, *A bear* is emphasized by being placed first.

Sentences that begin with such neutral words as *There is* and *There are* are not as forceful or interesting as those that begin with a subject.

Weak:	☐ There are a dozen crows in the cornfield.
Stronger:	☐ A dozen crows are in the cornfield.
Weak:	☐ There were fourteen persons stranded when the ferry broke down.
Stronger:	☐ Fourteen persons were stranded when the ferry broke down.

Unnecessary words sap vitality from sentences.

☐ He finally *tendered his resignation.*
(He finally resigned.)

☐ He was able to *make his escape* through a hole in the fence.
(He was able to escape through a hole in the fence.)

☐ The chief *is of the opinion* that the thieves made their getaway in a truck.
(The chief believes that the thieves made their getaway in a truck.)

☐ One man was injured and two cars damaged in an accident *which occurred* at the intersection of Hillcrest and Main streets about 5 p.m. yesterday.
(One man was injured and two cars damaged in an accident at the intersection of Hillcrest and Main streets about 5 p.m. yesterday.)

Repetition is often necessary for clarity and understanding and also for emphasis. This is particularly true in any attempt to explain complex matter or to persuade the reader to a particular point of view.

Repetition in such case, however, does not consist is saying the same words over and over, but rather in giving examples, telling stories that illustrate the idea, quoting experts, citing facts and figures, drawing conclusions, making predictions and presenting analogies.

The use of repetition calls for judgment. Too much may tire the reader; too little may leave him confused or bored. Complex matters need considerable repetition in varied forms; simple matters need little or no repetition.

The statement that emphasis can be obtained through repetition of important words and phrases, while true, needs some explanation. While repetition of identical words or phrases can provide emphasis in some instances, it generally detracts from the quality of writing and is an indication of unwillingness or inability to think of different ways of expressing the same ideas.

EXAMPLE

☐ The National Education Association has begun an investigation of the Baltimore public schools. The investigation was begun yesterday after local sanctions and a joint NEA-Maryland State Teachers Association warning failed to produce improvements in the educational conditions in the city.

The paragraph could be rewritten to avoid that repetition.

☐ The National Education Association has begun an investigation of the Baltimore public schools. The action was started yesterday after local sanctions and a joint NEA-Maryland State Teachers Association warning failed to produce improvements in the educational conditions in the city.

After you have reached this point in your study of grammar, it is unlikely that your writing will contain *sentence fragments* or *run-on sentences*, which are not acceptable in standard English.

■   **A sentence fragment is simply an incomplete sentence.**

EXAMPLES

The fragments are in italics.

Fragment: □   I had dinner at Barney's Steak House. *But I did not like the food.*

Corrected: □   I had dinner at Barney's Steak House, but I did not like the food.

Fragment: □   I won't go there again. *Because I don't like steak.*

Corrected: □   I won't go there again because I don't like steak.

■   **A run-on sentence is one in which two independent clauses (two complete sentences) are written as one but without a connective or a semicolon.**

EXAMPLES

Run-on sentence: □   The Fourth of July came on Friday this year, next year it will be on Sunday because of leap year.

Corrected: □   The Fourth of July came on Friday this year; next year it will be on Sunday because of leap year.

Run-on sentence: □   We usually celebrate the Fourth of July at the beach this year we are going to the park.

Corrected: □   We usually celebrate the Fourth of July at the beach, but this year we are going to the park.

■   **The first run-on sentence above is called a** *comma splice* **because two independent clauses (complete sentences) are connected by a comma, which is incorrect. When there is no connecting word or words, a semicolon is the only correct punctuation.**

■   The second run-on sentence above is called a *fused sentence* because it has no punctuation and no connecting word or words between the two independent clauses. Review the rules in Lesson 1.12 if you are not sure.

FOR PRACTICE

Rewrite these sentences to give emphasis to facts now subordinated.

1. The New York Yankees, who won the World Series for six consecutive years from 1949 to 1954, are an American League team.

2. Omega, a name given to one kind of subatomic particle, is the last letter of the Greek alphabet.

3. The grapes, which had been picked a week ago, were unfit to eat.

Rewrite this sentence to change the emphasis.

4. After three weeks of bad weather and mechanical difficulties, the space shuttle Columbia was successfully launched early this morning.

Rewrite this sentence by placing the fact of lesser importance in a subordinate position.

5. Dr. Henderson is the superintendent of schools; and he is polite, friendly, and well liked by the teachers.

Rewrite these sentences to change the emphasis.

6. I was sitting in the living room reading the morning newspaper when the earthquake began shaking the house.

7. The reference book was not in the library, so we could not complete the assignment.

8. He sat at the movies when his bicycle was stolen.

Underline the unnecessary word or words in each of these sentence.

9. The biscuits were small in size.

10. The elements were combined together to form a useful compound.

11. The procedure he adopted resulted in a new innovation in accounting.

12. The reason why he failed is not clear.

13. He failed because of the fact that he did not study his lessons.

Rewrite these sentences to make them more forceful.

14. There were five cows grazing in the pasture.

15. There are few schools in America that teach such exotic languages as Nepali and Urdu.

Rewrite these sentences to change the verbs to active voice.

16. The truck was being guarded by two men in uniform.

17. The message was delivered to us by Maria.

Punctuate these sentences correctly.

18. Dexter means on the right, sinister means on the left.

19. Myopia is nearsightedness, presbyopia is farsightedness.

20. Biennial is every other year biannual is twice a year.

6.5 FIGURES OF SPEECH ADD LIFE TO LANGUAGE.

Figures of speech add to the beauty of language by making it more vivid, colorful, and pleasing. Figures of speech are words and phrases that make imaginative comparisons. Grammarians list many kinds, the most common of which are *simile*, *metaphor*, *personification*, *hyperbole*, and *synedoche*.

Although it is not important to be able to identify figures of speech in order to use them effectively, some are listed here as examples.

■ A *simile* is a figure of speech that makes an *explicit comparison*, generally with the word *like* or *as*.

EXAMPLES

□ The event was as exciting as last year's calendar.
□ The figure mounts like a pocket calculator with the multiplication button stuck. — *Associated Press*.

■ A *metaphor* is a figure of speech similar to a simile, but without using the word *as* or *like*.

EXAMPLES

□ All the world's a stage, and all the men and women merely players.
□ Life's but a walking shadow, a poor player, that struts and frets his hour upon the stage, and then is heard no more. — *Shakespeare*

■ *Personification* is assigning personal qualities or human characteristics to inanimate objects.

EXAMPLES

□ The earth with *her thousand voices* praises God.
□ The waves *pounded* the rocky shore.
□ Love is patient; love is kind. Love is not jealous, it does not put on airs, it is not snobbish. — *I Corinthians 13:4*

■ A *hyperbole* is a figure of speech that greatly exaggerates. It states that something is much larger or smaller or better or worse than it really is.

EXAMPLES

- ☐ She was so thrilled that she was walking ten feet off the ground.
- ☐ Here once the embattled farmers stood, and fired the shot heard round the world. — *Ralph Waldo Emerson*
- ☐ Will all great Neptune's ocean wash this blood clean from my hand? — *Shakespeare*

■ A *synedoche* is a figure of speech in which a part is used for the whole or the whole for the part.

EXAMPLES

- ☐ Six *hands* were dismissed from the crew that day.
- ☐ Give us this day our daily *bread.*
- ☐ John has six *head* of hogs.

Figures of speech are an inseparable part of the English language. Poetry, the Bible, the works of Shakespeare, all good literature, are filled with imagery that helps make them more enjoyable to read. Here are some figures of speech gleaned from newspapers and magazines.

EXAMPLES

- ☐ As though it were a pie fight on a roller coaster

- ☐ A picket fence of ball point pens in his breast pocket

- ☐ As exciting as watching a weenie turn on a rotisserie

- ☐ With the exhilaration of a pack of beagles on the trail of a fox

- ☐ If Columbus had navigated the same way my wife does, he'd have ended up in South America

- ☐ Some changes have been as violent as electrical storms, while others creep slowly like sorghum syrup. — *TV Guide*

- ☐ He is putting in so many hours that he's scarcely getting the minimum wage. — *James Reston, New York Times*

- ☐ The dance team of three women and four men are, collectively, a card hand of seven aces. — *Time Magazine*

- ☐ I wandered lonely as a cloud. — *William Wordsworth*

- ☐ A tree that may in summer wear
  A nest of robins in her hair. — *Joyce Kilmer*

- ☐ As the lily among thorns, so is my love among the daughters. — *Songs of Solomon 2:2*

- ☐ Suffer not thy mouth to cause thy flesh to sin.
  — *Ecclesiastes 5:6*

■ **Figurative language differs from literal in that it consists of words and phrases used imaginatively rather that factually.**

EXAMPLES

Literal   ☐ I don't want anyone to weep when I die.

Figurative   ☐ May there be no moaning of the bar
               When I put out to sea.
               — *Alfred Tennyson*

Literal   ☐ A person can see many stars in the sky at night but only the sun during the day.

Figurative   ☐ The night has a thousand eyes,
               And the day but one.
               — *Francis William Bourdillon*

Some figures of speech, such as those below, have been used so much that they have become trite and should be avoided. Such overworked expressions are called *cliches*.

EXAMPLES

- ☐ slept like a log
- ☐ bury the hatchet
- ☐ in hot water
- ☐ sharp as a razor
- ☐ quick as a cat
- ☐ in one ear and out the other
- ☐ took the bull by the horns
- ☐ from the frying pan into the fire
- ☐ the picture of health
- ☐ on the tip of my tongue

As stated before, figures of speech should be imaginative and appropriate to the subject if they are to help the reader visualize what is being described and thus find what he is reading to be more interesting.

Another caveat is in regard to mixing figures of speech inappropriately. Grammarians call them "mixed metaphors."

EXAMPLES

- ☐ He straddled the fence on most issues while keeping his ear to the ground to gauge public opinion.
- ☐ He was at the helm of state as it marched to victory.
- ☐ When I smell a rat I nip it in the bud.

FOR PRACTICE

Underline the figurative language in these sentences.

1. He was bald as a bomb.
2. The tourist official was as unpleasant as the law allowed.
3. I seem to have thrown a rock into a hornets' nest.
4. The man was dumber than a box of rocks.
5. Their costumes blazed like sun-kindled autumn leaves.

For further practice, think of some comparison for

...slower than...
...as slow as...
...faster...
...as fast as...
...brighter than...
...as bright as...

and others.

ANSWERS

1. bald as a bomb
2. unpleasant as the law allowed
3. thrown a rock into a hornets' nest
4. dumber than a box of rocks
5. blazed like sun-kindled autumn leaves

REVIEW EXERCISES

Rewrite these sentences so that their structure will be parallel. With some, there are several possibilities.

1. She walked, talked, and was acting like a princess.

   ☐ _____

2. He likes to read books and writing letters to friends.

   ☐ _____

Rewrite these sentences so that the verbs are closer to their subjects.

3. *Neighbors* of Bettie Smith, who has spent most of her time in the past ten years feeding the hungry and helping the homeless find shelter on the south side of Chicago, *call* her an Angel of Mercy.

   ☐ _____

   _____

   _____

   _____

4. *The state's largest consumer group*, which has compiled a list of tabulated votes by state lawmakers over the past 20 years on bills related to consumer protection, *commended* Senator Hector Jones at a banquet last night for his support.

☐ _____
_____
_____
_____

Rewrite this sentence to make it active voice.

5. The workshop will be directed by Dr. James R. Vair.

☐ _____

Rewrite this sentence to make it passive voice.

6. The youngsters enjoyed playing on the sandy beach.

☐ _____

Rewrite these sentences to eliminate the shifts in voice.

7. Sarah watched the birds feeding, but she was not seen by them.

☐ _____

8. John attended classes for two weeks, but very little was learned by him.

☐ _____
_____

This sentence has a shift in voice. Rewrite it so it will be parallel.

9. The boards of directors of some companies might have re-thought earlier notions of raising dividends, but dividends were raised by many other boards of directors.

☐ _____
_____
_____

Rewrite this sentence to correct the shift in tense.

10. That morning John mowed the lawn while his brother sits reading a book.

☐ _____

_____

These sentences contain unrelated ideas. Can you add a unifying thought to each sentence and rewrite it so that the ideas are related?

11. He appeared sad and was well educated.

☐ _____

12. The two-party system is important, and members of the House of Representatives are elected for two-year terms.

☐ _____

_____

Rewrite this sentence to emphasize the number of marriage licenses issued.

13. Donald Mudd, clerk of courts, said yesterday that more than 300 marriage licenses were issued in Madison County last year.

☐ _____

_____

_____

Combine these two sentences into one complex sentence, subordinating the fact that the player is a left-handed pitcher.

14. Leonard Stark was traded to the New York Yankees yesterday. He has been a left-handed pitcher for the Pittsburgh Pirates.

☐ _____

_____

Rewrite this compound sentence as a complex sentence, subordinating where Wilson lives.

15. Kerry Wilson is my golf instructor, and he lives in Random Park.

    ☐ _____

    _____

Now rewrite that sentence, subordinating the fact that he is my golf instructor.

16. Kerry Wilson is my golf instructor, and he lives in Random Park.

    ☐ _____

    _____

Rewrite the second sentence to make clear to the reader that the italicized identification refers to Louis Garner, not to some other person.

17. Louis Garner has spent most of his life at sea. The *veteran ship captain* is a skillful navigator.

    ☐ _____

    _____

Rewrite this sentence to give it a more forceful beginning.

18. There are many persons who would like to have the ability to play the violin.

    ☐ _____

    _____

Underline the figure of speech in this sentence.

19. The news spread through the house faster than the smell of a cabbage dinner. — *Russell Baker*

Complete these sentences by using figures of speech.

20. The clouds were as dark as _____
and the thunder sounded like _____

ANSWERS

1. She walked, talked, and acted like a princess.
2. He likes to read books and to write letters to friends.
3. *Neighbors* of Bettie Smith *call* her an Angel of Mercy for spending most of her time in the past ten years feeding the hungry and helping the homeless find shelter on the south side of Chicago.

   Or, if you wish to emphasize her name, place it first in the sentence and use passive voice:

   Bettie Smith is called an Angel of Mercy by her neighbors for spending most of her time, etc.
4. One way to place subject and verb closer is to break this into two sentences:

   At a banquet last night, *the state's largest consumer group commended* Senator Hector Jones for his support. The group has tabulated votes by state lawmakers over the past 20 years on bills related to consumer protection.

   If you wish to emphasize his name by placing it first, use passive voice:

   Senator Hector Jones was commended at a banquet last night by the *state's largest consumer group* for his support. The group has tabulated votes by state lawmakers over the past 20 years on bills related to consumer protection.
5. Dr. James R. Vair will direct the workshop.
6. Playing on the beach was enjoyed by the youngsters.
7. Sarah watched the birds feeding, but they did not see her.

8. John attended classes for two weeks, but he learned very little.

9. The boards of directors of some companies might have re-thought earlier notions of raising dividends, but many other boards of directors raised dividends.

10. That morning John mowed the lawn while his brother sat reading a book.

11. He appeared sad; but when he spoke, he gave the impression of being well educated.

12. The two-party system is important in providing a choice to the voters, a choice that occurs every two years in the election of members of the House of Representatives.

13. More than 300 marriage licenses were issued in Madison County last year, Donald Mudd, clerk of courts, said yesterday.

14. Leonard Stark, who has been a left-handed pitcher for the Pittsburgh Pirates, was traded to the New York Yankees yesterday.

15. Kerry Wilson, who lives in Random Park, is my golf instructor.

16. Kerry Wilson, who is my golf instructor, lives in Random Park.

17. Mr. Garner, the veteran ship captain, is a skillful navigator.

18. Many persons would like to have the ability to play the violin.

19. faster than the smell of a cabbage dinner

20. Here you have many choices. Possibilities: dark as midnight; dark as pitchblende; thunder sounded like cannon; like a bombardment; like the fury of battle. And you can think of better ones than these.

GRAMMATICAL TERMS

active voice - form of the verb in which the subject is the doer of the act or performs the action: John caught the ball. The subject, John, did the act. See voice.

adjective - a word that modifies, describes, or limits a noun or a pronoun: tall man, beautiful music, red rose. One of the eight parts of speech.

adjective clause - a dependent clause that modifies a noun or a pronoun: The man *who came to dinner* is the mayor. The dependent adjective clause modifies *man*, which is the subject of the sentence.

adverb - a word that modifies a verb, an adjective, or another adverb: He played skillfully. The adverb *skillfully* modifies the verb *played* by telling how he played. One of the eight parts of speech.

adverbial clause - a dependent clause that modifies a verb, an adjective, or another adverb, often the verb in the sentence: We will clean the house *before the guests arrive*. That dependent adverbial clause modifies the verb *will clean* by telling when it will be done.

agreement - the accord of pronouns with their antecedents in person, number, and gender, and of verbs with their subjects in person and number.

antecedent - the word, phrase, or clause referred to by a pronoun: Jennifer lost her purse. The antecedent of the pronoun *her* is *Jennifer*.

apostrophe - a punctuation mark that is like a comma in appearance but goes at the top of the line (') and is used to show possession, plurals of letters and numbers, and the omission of a letter or letters in contractions: *Sam's farm, P's* and *Q's, isn't.*

appositive - a noun or a noun phrase that identifies or explains the noun it follows: Paul Anderson, a *successful businessman*, owns the bakery in our town.

article - the words *a, an,* and *the* are called articles and usually function as adjectives.

auxiliary verb - a helping verb added to the main verb to assist in expressing various ideas: *would* go, *shall* build, *are* coming, *could have* won.

case - the form or position a noun or a pronoun takes to indicate its relations to other words in the sentences. Only nouns and pronouns have case. The cases are nominative, objective, and possessive. The form of a noun remains the same in the nominative and objective cases; but an apostrophe and sometimes the letter s are added in the possessive case. The form of personal pronouns, however, changes for each case according to the function of the pronoun in the sentence.

Nominative	☐	*He* is my brother.
Objective	☐	I like *him*.
Possessive	☐	This ball is *his*.

clause - a group of grammatically related words that contains a subject and a verb. An independent clause, also known as the main clause or principal clause, can stand alone as a sentence as it expresses a complete thought. A dependent clause, also known as a subordinate clause, cannot stand alone as it does not express a complete thought and always appears in complex sentences.

collective noun - a noun that names a group: *family, committee, company, herd, flock.*

comma - a punctuation mark (,) used within the sentence to separate parts in order to add clarity and meaning.

comma splice - a comma splice occurs when two independent clauses are incorrectly connected with a comma. Only a semicolon can join independent clauses to form compound sentences. See run-on sentence.

Incorrect:	☐	Gertrude's favorite vacation area is Hilton Head, Louise prefers to go to the Bahamas.
Correct:	☐	Gertrude's favorite vacation area is Hilton Head, but Louise prefers to go to the Bahamas.
Correct:	☐	Gertrude's favorite vacation area is Hilton Head; Louise prefers to go to the Bahamas.

common noun - the name for all of the same kind of persons, places, and things: *tree*, *dog*, *country*, *happiness*. Common nouns are not capitalized as are proper nouns.

comparative degree - comparison between two persons or things. See comparison.

comparison - the variation in form of an adjective or an adverb to indicate different degrees of quality. The three degrees of comparison are positive, comparative, and superlative. The positive degree of comparison refers to only one, the comparative to two, and the superlative to more than two: *good, better, best; quickly, more quickly, most quickly.*

complement - to complete. Not to be confused with compliment, which means to praise. See predicate complement.

complete predicate - all of the words that comprise the predicate, including the verb and its modifiers, as distinguished from the simple predicate, which includes only the verb: Our Uncle Jose / is *a skilled craftsman*. See simple predicate.

complete subject - all the words in the sentence that comprise the subject, as distinguished from the simple subject which includes only the key noun or pronoun: *The man whose horse won the race* / is my uncle.

complex sentence - a sentence that contains an independent clause and one or more dependent (subordinate) clauses: The man *whose horse won the race* is my uncle.
  A simple sentence + a dependent clause = a complex sentence.

compound - something formed by combining parts. In grammar there are compound words, compound subjects, compound predicates, and compound sentences.

compound-complex sentence - a sentence formed by joining a simple sentence and a complex sentence or two or more complex sentences: We had planned to go fishing that day; but when the rain began, we decided to remain at home.

A simple sentence + a complex sentence = a compound-complex sentence.

A complex sentence + a complex sentence = a compound-complex sentence.

compound sentence - a sentence formed by joining two or more simple sentences to form one: The rain stopped before noon, and the sun shone all afternoon.

compound predicate - two or more predicates connected as a unit in a sentence: The flowering plants *grew rapidly* and *blossomed abundantly.*

compound subject - two or more subjects connected as a unit in a sentence: *The ice cream* and *the cake* were delicious as a dessert.

conjugation - naming the principal parts of a verb, as present, past, and past participle: move, moved, moved; ring, rang, rung.

conjunction - a word or words used to connect words, phrases, and clauses to form grammatical units. One of the eight parts of speech. See connective.

conjunctive adverb - an adverb used to connect independent clauses to form compound sentences: *besides, accordingly, furthermore, however, also,* etc. He went to bed early that night; *however,* he could not sleep. When a conjunctive adverb is used as a connective in a compound sentence, it is preceded by a semicolon and usually followed by a comma.

connective - a word or words that join two or more clauses to form complex sentences, compound sentences, and compound-complex sentences. There are six kinds: *Subordinating conjunctions* connect dependent clauses to independent clauses to form complex sentences, and *relative pronouns* introduce dependent clauses in complex sentences. *Coordinating conjunctions, correlative conjunctions, conjunctive adverbs,* and *transitional phrases* are used to connect independent clauses to form compound sentences.

contraction - the combination of two words to form one word, with one or more letters omitted and an apostrophe indicating the omission: is not = isn't; we will = we'll; will not = won't.

coordinating conjunction - coordinate means equal rank. A coordinating conjunction is used to connect or link not only sentences but also words and groups of words of equal rank. The coordinating conjunctions are *and*, *but*, *or*, *for*, *so*, *yet*, and *nor*.

correlative conjunction - pairs of words that serve the same function as coordinating conjunctions: *either...or, both...and, neither...nor, not only...but also*. *Both* sisters were in Europe, *and* their father lay ill at home.

dangling modifier - a modifying word, phrase, or clause in a sentence in which it is not clear what the modifier refers to: The man was trying to repair his automobile *with a broken finger*. The modifying phrase in that sentence is said to "dangle" because its placement makes it refer incorrectly to *automobile*. It should read: The man *with the broken finger* was trying to repair his automobile.

declarative sentence - sentence that declares, that makes a statement, that tells something: The Detroit Tigers won the World Series in 1984.

declension - naming the variation of nouns to denote number and case and naming the variation of pronouns to denote person, number, gender, and case.

demonstrative adjective - *this*, *that*, *these*, and *those* are called demonstrative adjectives when they come immediately before nouns: *this* man, *that* dish, *these* boys, *those* papers. *This* dress is similar to *that* dress.

demonstrative pronouns - *this*, *that*, *these*, and *those* are called demonstrative pronouns when they point to a particular person, place, thing, or group: *This* is the best melon I have ever tasted. *That* was his son who won the prize. Note that a demonstrative pronoun begins the sentence, and is the subject of the verb; demonstrative adjectives modify nouns.

dependent clause - a group of grammatically related words that contains a subject and a verb but does not express a complete thought and thus cannot stand alone as a sentence. Dependent clauses are also called subordinate clauses.

direct address - the person or persons or group or thing spoken to, always separated from the rest of the sentence by a comma or commas: Friends, we will soon be there. I want you, Carlos, to go with me.

direct object - the person or thing that receives the action of a transitive verb: Juan hit the *ball*. In that sentence, *the ball* is the direct object as it received the action of the verb *hit*. Also called *object complement*.

ellipsis - the omission of one or more words in a sentence, marked by three periods or dots: We arrived early...but no one met us. Ellipses are commonly used when words or sentences are omitted in exact quotations of printed matter.

exclamation point - a punctuation mark (!) used at the end of an exclamatory sentence, after one or more exclamatory words, and after an imperative sentence that contains an emphatic command. It is also called an exclamation mark.

exclamatory sentence - a sentence that expresses strong feeling and is punctuated with an exclamation point at the end: Stop that foolishness!

figurative language - words that carry other than their ordinary meaning: the opposite of literal language: I wandered lonely as a cloud.

figure of speech - expressive use of the language in which words are used in other than their literal sense. Among figures of speech are the simile, metaphor, personification, hyperbole, and synedoche. Metaphor from Shakespeare: Life's but a walking shadow.

fragment - See sentence fragment.

fused sentence - a compound sentence in which the independent clauses are joined by no punctuation or incorrect punctuation or lack a connective: The band began playing music for a polka soon the floor was crowded with dancers. Correct: The band began playing music for a polka; soon the floor was crowded with dancers. Also correct: The band began playing music for a polka, and soon the floor was crowded with dancers.

gender - classification of nouns and pronouns as masculine, feminine, and neuter.

gerund - a verb that ends in *ing* but functions as a noun: *Walking* is good exercise.

grammar - the study of the rules that govern the accepted structure of a language.

helping verb - See auxiliary verb.

imperative mood - form of the verb used in a sentence that makes a request or gives a command: (You) Wish me luck.

imperative sentence - a sentence that makes a request or gives a command: Bring me the book. If an imperative sentence contains strong feeling as in a command, it is followed by an exclamation point: Stop right there! Usually the subject, You, is implied or understood.

indefinite pronoun - a pronoun that does not refer to any particular person, place, or thing: *none, most, all, everyone, each,* etc.

independent clause - a group of grammatically related words that contains one or more subjects, one or more verbs, and expresses a complete thought. An independent clause can stand alone as a complete sentence, or it may be part of a complex sentence or a compound sentence or a compound-complex sentence. An independent clause is also called a *main clause* or a *principal clause* in a complex sentence.

indicative mood - form of the verb used in a declarative sentence, in a sentence that makes a statement or tells something: Labor Day falls on the first Monday in September.

indirect object - the person or thing for whom or for which or to whom or to which an act is done. It usually comes just before the direct object in a sentence: John gave *him* the ball. The word *him* is the indirect object; *ball* is the direct object. The sentence can be restated so that the indirect object becomes the object of a preposition: John gave the ball *to him*.

infinitive - a verbal formed by a verb preceded by the word *to*, which is the "sign of the infinitive": *to go*, *to believe*, *to wander*, *to guess*.

interjection - an exclamation, or a word or words "thrown in," with no grammatical relation to the remainder of the sentence. It may express strong feeling: Well! Oh! The interjection is one of the eight parts of speech.

interrogative pronoun - a pronoun that begins an interrogative sentence. The interrogative pronouns are *who*, *whom*, *whose*, *which*, *whoever*, *whatever*, *whichever*, *whomever*, and *that*: *Whose* turn is it?

interrogative sentence - a sentence that asks a question: When will you be ready to go?

intransitive verb - a verb that does not require an object to complete the meaning of the sentence: She *laughed*. Linking verbs are intransitive but require predicate complements (predicate nominatives or predicate adjectives) but not objects to complete the meaning: She *was happy*. In that sentence the linking verb is *was* and the predicate complement is *happy*.

irregular verb - a verb that does not form its past tense and past participle with the addition of *d*, *ed* or *t*: *drink*, *drank*, *drunk*; *fly*, *flew*, *flown*.

linking verb - a verb that links the subject to the predicate complement, which is either a predicate nominative or a predicate adjective. Linking verbs include such words as *feel*, *smell*, *taste*, *look*, and *seem* as well as all forms of the verb *be*, such as *is*, *was*, *were*: Juan *was* an engineer. Mary *is* happy.

main clause - the independent or principal clause in a complex sentence: *I will tell him* when he arrives.

metaphor - a figure of speech that makes a comparison, usually without using the words *as* or *like*: All the world's a stage. She is a tiger.

misplaced modifier - a modifier placed in a sentence in such manner as to give an unintended meaning: He was fined $50 for a traffic violation *in municipal court this morning*. With the modifying phrase placed as it is in that sentence, the sentence appears to say that the traffic violation was committed in court. To be correct, the phrase should come immediately after *fined $50*: He was fined $50 in municipal court this morning for a traffic violation.

mixed metaphor - unrelated comparisons in the same sentence: Always the politician, he straddled the fence on issues while keeping his ear to the ground for public opinion.

modifier - a word or words that describe, explain, or limit another word, phrase, or clause. Adjectives and adverbs and adjective and adverb phrases and clauses are modifiers.

mood - form of a verb that indicates whether the action or state it denotes is true or a command or a possibility or a wish. The three modes of verbs are *indicative*, used in sentences that make statements or ask questions; *imperative*, used in sentences that give commands or make requests; and *subjunctive*, used in sentences that express possibilities or wishes or conditions contrary to fact.

nominative case - the case of a noun or a pronoun when it is the subject of a verb, a predicate nominative, in apposition with a noun or a pronoun in the nominative case, and the object of the infinitive *to be* when the infinitive has no subject.

noun - name of a person, place, thing, or idea. One of the eight parts of speech.

number - the form of a noun, pronoun, demonstrative adjective, or verb that indicates whether it is singular or plural.

object - a noun or a pronoun or a group of words used as a noun that is the object of a verb (receiver of the action of the verb), the indirect object of a verb, the object of a preposition, the subject or object of an infinitive, or the object of a gerund.

object complement - the person or thing that receives the action of a transitive verb, necessary to complete the sentence: He drank *the water*. Luis caught *a fish*. Each italicized word is an object complement, the receiver of the action of the verb and is in the objective case. Also called *direct object*.

object of a preposition - a noun or a pronoun that completes the prepositional phrase. It is always in the objective case: I gave the book to *her*. We saw the mountains behind *them*.

objective case - one of the forms a noun or a pronoun takes to show how it functions in a sentence: We gave *her* the money. We complimented *him* on his work.

parallel structure - similar grammatical construction in a sentence: The car r*an well* on level roads, but it *sputtered* going upgrade. A shift in voice can result in a lack of parallel structure: A person *can work* hard all day picking tomatoes, but very little money is earned. See shift.

parenthetical expression - a word or words not essential to the meaning of the sentence and set off from the rest of the sentence by a comma or commas: *In fact*, I hardly knew him. He was, t*o tell the truth,* an undesirable resident in the housing complex.

participle - a verb form called a verbal that functions as an adjective: They ran before the *spreading* storm. The present participle ends in *ing*; the past participle of regular verbs ends in *d, ed* or *t*.

participial phrase - a phrase that begins with a participle and functions as an adjectival modifier in a sentence: *Frightened by the noise*, the dog ran away. The participle is *Frightened*; the phrase modifies the noun *dog*.

parts of speech - The eight parts of speech are noun, pronoun, verb, adverb, adjective, preposition, conjunction, and interjection. The manner in which a word functions in a sentence determines what part of speech it is.

passive voice - the voice in which the verb makes its subject the receiver of the action: The ball *was caught* by John. Only transitive verbs can be in passive voice.

past participle - form of the verb used in the perfect tenses: *had played, have come, has fled*. A past participle without the auxiliary may also function in a sentence as an adjective: *Worried*, he could not sleep. In that sentence the italicized past participle modifies the pronoun *he*.

person - form of the pronoun and accompanying verb which shows whether it is the person or persons speaking (first person: I am, we are), or the person or persons spoken to (second person: You are), or the person or persons spoken of (third person: he is, she is, it is, they are).

personal pronoun - the form of a pronoun which shows its person. The singular nominative personal pronouns are *I* for first person; *you* for second person; and *he*, *she*, and *it* for third person. See page 72.

personification - a figure of speech in which human attributes are given to inanimate objects: October *dressed in her autumn finery*.

phrase - a group of words that modifies another word in the sentence but does not itself form a sentence as it has no subject and no predicate and does not express a complete thought:

Absolute phrase	° *The dishes washed*, we retired to the living room.
Appositive phrase	° My uncle, *an avid bridge player*, lives in St. Louis.
Gerund phrase	° Most of the work consisted of *washing our clothes*.
Infinitive phrase	° We waited for him *to tell us the story*.
Noun phrase	° *Enormous dark clouds* were building up in the west.
Participial phrase	° The flowers *blooming in the garden* were beautiful.
Prepositional phrase	° The books were placed *on the shelves*.
Verb phrase	° The rain *had been falling* all morning.

positive degree - in comparison the positive degree states a quality without comparing it with another of the same class: The flowers are pretty.

possessive case - the form nouns and pronouns take to show possession or ownership: *John's* hat, *my* house.

possessive pronoun - a personal pronoun that shows possession or ownership: *my* pen, *her* dress, *your* automobile, *their* misfortune.

predicate - that part of a sentence that tells about the subject: A full moon / *was shining that night.*

predicate complement - that part of the predicate after the verb necessary to complete the sentence. The three kinds of predicate complements are predicate nominative, predicate adjective, and predicate object or object complement: Morris is a *physician.* He is *skillful.* He treated *me.*

preposition - one of the eight parts of speech, it is the first word in a prepositional phrase. A preposition expresses a relation to another word in the sentence and governs the case of the noun or pronoun called its object: *into* the water, *beside* the table, *with* her.

prepositional phrase - a phrase that begins with a preposition, ends with a noun or pronoun, and is either an adverbial or an adjectival modifier.

principal parts of verbs - forms of a verb from which all other forms can be derived. The four principal parts are the present tense, which is the base form, the past tense, the present participle, and the past participle: *walk, walked, walking, (has) walked.*

pronoun - a word that stands for a noun, that may be used in place of a noun: Janice told us *her* address.

proper adjective - adjective derived from a proper noun and capitalized: *Spanish* music, the *American* way, *Swiss* cheese.

proper noun - the name of a specific person, place, or thing: *China, Chicago, Tuesday, Irving Berlin.* Proper nouns are always capitalized.

reciprocal pronoun - a pronoun that shows a mutual relationship: *each other, one another.* We should help *one another.*

reflexive pronoun - a pronoun that ends with *self* and refers back to its antecedent: *Louise* assured *herself* that she was right.

regular verb - a verb that forms the past tense and the past participle by adding *d* or *ed* or *t: talk, talked, (has) talked.* See irregular verbs.

restrictive clause - a dependent clause in a complex sentence that is essential to the meaning of the sentence: The car *that he drove* is a Ford.

run-on sentence - a compound sentence with incorrect punctuation or lack of punctuation or use of an improper connective joining the independent clauses. See *comma splice* and *fused sentence.*

sentence - a complete thought expressed in words. Every complete sentence contains one or more subjects and one or more verbs.

sentence fragment - a group of words, such as a dependent clause or a participial phrase, that does not express a complete thought: If you can come. Watching the ball game.

shift - the change from one tense, voice, mood, subject, person, or number to another in the same sentence.

Shift in tense	☐	When she *heard* the story, she *believes* in miracles.
Correct	☐	When she heard the story, she believed in miracles.
Shift in voice	☐	William and I *went* fishing, but no fish *were caught.*
Correct	☐	William and I went fishing, but we caught no fish.
Shift in mood	☐	*Get* all of your tools together and then you *should begin* work.
Correct	☐	Get all your tools together and then begin work.

Shift in subject	☐	*Mario* planted corn, and *tomatoes* were
(and voice)		raised by him.
Correct	☐	Mario planted corn and raised tomatoes.
Shift in number	☐	Cora ate *an apple*; *they* were delicious.
Correct	☐	Cora ate an apple; it was delicious.

simile - a figure of speech that makes a comparison using *like* or *as*: He is *as strong as an ox*.

simple predicate - the complete verb in the predicate: All of the money *was lost* in gambling.

simple subject - the key noun or pronoun in the subject without its modifiers: The flowering *plant* we saw yesterday is a columbine.

simple sentence - a complete sentence that has no dependent clauses.

split infinitive - an infinitive with one or more words between the sign *to* and the verb: to *strongly* believe, to *awkwardly* dance.

subject - what the sentence (the thought) is about.

subject complement - the same as predicate complement except that this term applies only to the predicate adjective which modifies the subject and to the predicate nominative which renames the subject. See predicate complement.

subjunctive mood - form of a verb used in expressing a wish and in a statement contrary to fact. Contrary to fact: If I *were* happy, I would smile. Wish: I wish my sister *were* interested in college.

subordinate clause - a dependent clause, which is a group of grammatically related words that has a subject and a verb but does not express a complete thought and therefore does not constitute a complete sentence, but rather is a part of a complex sentence.

superlative degree - comparison among more than two persons, places, or things. See comparison.

syntax - the way words are put together to form phrases, clauses, and sentences.

tense - time expressed by verbs; form of verbs that indicates when a condition existed or an act occurred. The simple tenses are present, past, and future; the perfect tenses are present perfect, past perfect, and future perfect.

transitive verb - a verb that requires an object to complete its meaning; it is a verb that tells of an action by an agent upon an object: Juan *caught* the ball. In that sentence *the ball* received the action of the transitive verb *caught*.

transitional phrase - two or more words used as a connective in joining sentences together to form compound and compound-complex sentences: He campaigned energetically for the office; *at the same time*, he had doubts that he would win the election.

verb - the part of speech that asserts an action or assumes a relation and is an essential part of every sentence. One kind of verb indicates an action: *run*, *speak*, *walk*. The other indicates only a relationship or a condition: *was*, *have*, *are*.

verbal - a verb form that functions as a noun or an adjective or an adverb. The three verbals are *infinitives*, *participles*, and *gerunds*.

voice -the property of a verb that shows whether its subject is the doer of an action or the receiver of an action, whether the subject is acting or being acted upon. Active voice: Pedro *caught* the ball. Passive voice: The ball *was caught* by Pedro. Only verbs that express action can have voice.

INDEX